KING OF THE JEWS

KING OF THE JEWS

Why the Bible – and all history – points to Jesus

Charles Gardner

Christian Publications International

*First published in Great Britain by
Christian Publications International
an imprint of
Buy Research Ltd.
PO Box 212 SAFFRON WALDEN CB10 2UU*

Cover design by Justyn Hall at J8 Creative
Email: justyn@J8creative.co.uk

Online references cited in this book are correct at the time of publication.
Online material may be deleted or reassigned at the copyright holder's
discretion. Readers are reminded that such material may be transient in duration.

www.christian-publications-int.com

ISBN 978-1-78926-510-1

Printed in England by Imprint Digital, Exeter
and worldwide by Ingram Spark

To my beloved wife Linda, a tower of strength, encouragement and wisdom.

Contents

Foreword   9

Introduction   11

1. A Double Blessing   13

2. Jesus in the Tanakh   21

3. Dead Sea Comes to Life!   33

4. Total Integrity (a study of Nathanael, John 1.43-51)   41

5. The Joy of Job   47

6. Two Beautiful Women (Ruth & Esther)   61

7. Bibi and the Bible   71

8. An Upside-down Media   79

9. Battle for Truth Continues   85

10. Fulfilment of the Feasts   91

11. Light in the Darkness   99

12. Jews Follow Jesus   107

13. Arab-Jewish Harmony   127

14. A Gentile Perspective   139

15. Christians Back Israel   149

16. Sign of the Times   157

17. Germany's 9/11   171

18. Britain's Role   179

19. The View From Israel   195

20. A Solid Foundation   205

Epilogue – The Incurable Romantic   219

Bibliography   224

About the Author   225

FOREWORD

by Dr Frederick Wright

Charles Gardner brings a refreshingly relevant look at the Kingship of Yeshua. Most books dealing with this subject tend simply to mine for so-called 'proof texts' from the Tanakh (Old Testament) to illustrate the Messiahship of Yeshua and just leave it there.

The current work departs from such endeavours in a refreshingly dynamic way. The fast-paced narrative style brings the subject matter from the Tanakh, through the New Testament, right up to the present day.

The strength of this most relevant work is that it interfaces with the times in which we live and challenges us to recognise that Yeshua is indeed not only 'King of the Jews' but the author and perfecter of our faith (Hebrews 12:1-3).

Author and theologian Fred Wright has been actively involved for over three decades in helping Jewish people suffering persecution in many parts of the world to make Aliyah by immigrating to their national homeland. He recounts some of his extraordinary adventures in his latest book, A Banner to the Nations, *published by Chesed Publishing and available from Amazon and* www.lulu.com

A former head-teacher, lecturer and pastor, Fred lives in Colchester, Essex, with his wife Maria.

INTRODUCTION – IT'S ALL ABOUT JESUS!

My purpose in writing this book is to explain how, in many and various ways, Jesus fulfilled the Tanakh (what Christians refer to as the Old Testament). This is by no means an exhaustive treatment of the subject – more an introduction, leaving room for much more digging – as I examine both familiar and unlikely passages.

Right at the beginning of our Lord's ministry at the age of 30, one of his first disciples, Philip, sought out Nathanael and told him: *We have found the one Moses wrote about in the Law, and about whom the prophets also wrote – Jesus of Nazareth, son of Joseph* (John 1.45; and see Deuteronomy 18.15).

At the end of his earthly ministry, following his resurrection, Jesus drew alongside two friends on the road to Emmaus. Noting their despondency over hopes of redemption seemingly dashed, he scolded them: *How foolish you are, and how slow of heart to believe all that the prophets have spoken! Did not the Messiah have to suffer these things and then enter his glory? And beginning with Moses and all the Prophets, he explained to them what was said in all the Scriptures concerning himself* (Luke 24.25-27). He later reminded a larger group of disciples: *This is what I told you while I was still with you: Everything must be fulfilled that is written about me in the Law of Moses, the Prophets and the Psalms* (Luke 24.44). I will elaborate on this later.

He also said: *If you believed Moses, you would believe me, for he wrote about me* (John 5.46). A fairly obvious example of this comes from Deuteronomy 18.15, where Moses writes:

The Lord your God will raise up for you a prophet like me from among your own brothers. You must listen to him. A promise perfectly fulfilled when Jesus appeared with Moses and Elijah on the Mt of Transfiguration and a voice from above announced: *This is my Son, whom I love. Listen to him!*

Jesus (*Yeshua* in Hebrew) made it abundantly clear that much of the Old Testament was effectively all about him! And at the conclusion of the Acts of the Apostles, we read how Paul explained about the kingdom of God, and how *from the Law of Moses and from the Prophets he tried to persuade them about Jesus.*

So I wanted to explore this further – first, for the benefit of Yeshua's brothers in the flesh, the Jewish people, but also so that others may discover the precious riches of Christianity's Hebraic roots.

I will also include testimonies bearing out the truth of the gospel (good news) Jesus came to bring and, because the Christian faith is indelibly linked with the land and people of Israel (ancient and modern), I will also be looking at the responsibilities that these matters bring to those who purport to follow the God of Abraham, Isaac and Jacob.

Charles Gardner
Doncaster, South Yorkshire
December 2019

CHAPTER 1 – A DOUBLE BLESSING

How God shows his love to both Jews and Gentiles

It was always God's purpose that the Jews should be a blessing to the world. But it was also his purpose that Gentiles should be a blessing to the Jews (Genesis 12.3). After all, God is supremely interested in relationships. And my family tree has been blessed on both counts – by both Jews and Gentiles, that is.

My Jewish ancestors suffered under the dreadful persecution of the Spanish Inquisition; they fled from Spain to Portugal and were eventually banished from the latter several centuries ago. Fortunately, they escaped with their lives and subsequently became a blessing to England, South Africa and the Americas. My half-Jewish grandmother was actually born in Jamaica, but moved to England upon marrying an English army officer. And it was while living with her in Hampstead, London, that I had an encounter with Jesus and became a born-again Christian.

I am also greatly indebted to Gentile Christians for, on my father's side of the family, I am a fifth generation South African owing our survival there to the kindness of Dutch-Afrikaans Christians who took in my orphaned great-grandfather, also Charles, along with his siblings following the untimely death of their parents. Charles was subsequently brought up in the beautiful Cape Dutch parsonage of the Rev Andrew Murray, a Scotsman who obeyed God's call to help pastor the dispersed Dutch-Reformed Christians who had fled the repressive restrictions of the British at Cape Town, and were left somewhat harassed and helpless, without shepherds, deep into the South African interior. Rev Murray initially went to Holland to learn the language. Though he and his wife Maria had 16 children of their own, including the more famous revivalist and devotional writer Andrew Murray Jnr., they also felt it their duty to look after widows and orphans, as the Bible instructs us (see James 1.27) and I am eternally grateful for that.

I have since discovered the reality that Jesus came both for the Jew and the Gentile. And I will begin with my thoughts on a New Testament passage from the Gospel of Matthew (chapter 8, verses 1-17). The setting is by the shores of Galilee, perhaps my favourite place in all the world, where my wife and I were privileged to be in the autumn of 2017. Having just delivered what is widely acclaimed as the greatest sermon ever preached (the Sermon on the Mount), Jesus came down from the mountain followed by large crowds who were reportedly "amazed" at his teaching – in perfect fulfilment, I believe, of the prophet Isaiah's statement: *How beautiful upon the mountains are the feet of those who bring good news...* (Isa 52.7). A beautiful setting indeed, but how much more beautiful is the God of Israel whose ways are so majestically described in that awesome sermon – full of grace and truth, mercy and love for undeserved sinners, yet also a priceless treasure of all truth, righteousness and judgment. Jerusalem may be the city of the great King, and Israel the land of milk and honey, but how much more wonderful is the God of Israel himself!

Jesus was not a crowd-pleaser; he was interested in individuals, and the work the Father gave him to do. As he descended the so-called Mt of Beatitudes, a leper came and knelt before him, at which point I imagine that the crowd backed off – believing that leprosy was very contagious. To their amazement, Jesus touched him – and healed him! Can you imagine how that made him feel? He had probably not been touched, even by close relatives, for a long time. It was the first specific healing recorded in the New Testament, and hugely significant too I believe. I understand there is a rabbinical tradition holding that the healing of a leper would be a sign of the Messiah's coming,[1] which is perhaps why Rabbi Jesus told the man not to tell anyone, but to testify to the priest and *offer the gift Moses commanded* (see Leviticus 14), presumably some 70 miles away in Jerusalem. At any rate, when the imprisoned John the Baptist needed reassurance of Christ's credentials, Jesus said: *Go back and report to John what you hear and see: The blind receive sight, the lame walk, those who have leprosy are cleansed…* (Matthew 11.4f). Certainly, many Bible teachers say (though without giving reference) that the rabbis would have known such a healing was a sign of the Messiah. In any case, Jesus was clearly giving opportunity for the religious leaders to acknowledge that the Messiah had come and so encourage the general populace to believe. Of course the healing was also a sign of the gospel itself – the announcement of good news to the poor in fulfilment of Isaiah's prophecy (Isa 61).

Jesus' instruction that the leper show himself to the priest also obviously demonstrates that the man was a Jew; it is worth noting that Galilee at the time was quite heavily populated by Gentiles, and probably not just Roman soldiers. Nearby Tiberius, for example, was very much a Roman city to which Jews hardly ever ventured. It was not for nothing that, 700 years earlier, Isaiah referred prophetically to *Galilee of the nations* where *the people walking in darkness have seen a great light* (see Isa 9.1f).

I believe that the healing of the Jewish leper was specifically meant as a testimony to the priests that Messiah is among them; that Jesus had come, not to abolish the Law but to fulfil it (as he had just explained on the mount – Matthew 5.17), and for the lost sheep of the house of Israel (Matthew 10.6). In a wider sense, it seemed he was reversing the curse on a broken world infected by sin. He had come for the sick, not for those who claimed to be righteous (Luke 5.31) – and, specifically, he had come for the Jew.

But he had also come for the Gentile. The very next person he helped was a Roman centurion, whose servant was sick. This happened as he entered Capernaum, where much of his ministry was to be carried out. The occupying officer recognised Jesus' authority, knowing from experience that those under his command would instantly obey his every word; and that all Jesus had to do was *just say the word* and his servant would be healed. He recognised that he did not deserve to have the Rabbi come under his roof; that the same God who spoke the heavens into existence was perfectly capable of healing his servant. Great humility from one who, technically-speaking, could have given orders to the Jewish rabbi. But even greater faith for his absolute trust in the word of God, causing Jesus to say: *Truly I tell you, I have not found anyone in Israel with such great faith* (Matthew 8.10). And of course, as Jesus and his apostles were later to expound, acceptance into the kingdom of God would only come through faith.

This was in marked contrast to the lack of faith expressed in Jesus' home town (Nazareth), which was the reason he was unable to perform many miracles there (Mark 6.4, Matthew 11.20-24). Jesus even pronounced that Capernaum (to which he later moved) would one day *go down to the depths* because of its rejection of him – perfectly fulfilled in time as the town is only a heap of ruins today.

And so it was that the great Apostle Paul, though as Jewish as it was possible to be, felt especially called to share the gospel with the Gentiles and, to the early believers in Rome (a mixture of Jews and Gentiles), he stated unequivocally: *I am not ashamed of the gospel, for it is the power of God unto salvation for all who believe; to the Jew first, and also to the Gentile* (Romans 1.16).

Also hugely significant is the fact that the centurion was a god-fearing man who had great respect for the Jews and even built a synagogue for them (as we see from Luke's account of this incident in chapter 7 of his Gospel). His blessing of the Jews was a key to his own blessing from God (Gen 12.3). I believe this could well have been the same centurion as the one Luke mentioned in Acts 10, who also loved the Jews and became the means of blessing to the entire Gentile world when his family received the Holy Spirit through the preaching of Peter. I believe it is also significant that Luke, thought to have been the only Gentile writer of the New Testament (or indeed of the entire Bible), should have noted the connection between blessing Jews and being blessed. Of course it was a great shock to Peter, as Luke correctly observes, that Gentiles should also be blessed with the Holy Spirit of God in this way!

And so the gospel – to the Jew first – was now also offered to the Gentile. We hear much about amazing grace, but Jesus was amazed by this man's faith. The only other time he is recorded as having been amazed was by the lack of faith in his home town Nazareth (see Mark 6.6).

I wonder too if our Lord was also looking ahead to a day when faithful Gentiles would make an extraordinary mark on the world. In Yorkshire alone in recent centuries (I am biased because I live there) I can immediately think of three men who changed the world through their faith in Jesus: William Wilberforce from Hull, who successfully campaigned for the abolition of slavery; Barnsley's Hudson Taylor, to whom millions of Chinese Christians owe their salvation, and Bradford plumber Smith Wigglesworth, who raised 14 people from the dead as he helped to pioneer the modern-day Pentecostal movement which had such a profound impact on twentieth century Christianity.

In addition, the last 500 years have seen the Bible translated into virtually every language across the globe – at great personal cost through martyrs like William Tyndale (for daring to translate the Bible into English) and a teenager called Mary Jones, whose 26-mile walk over the mountains to purchase a Welsh Bible with six years' worth of savings inspired the founding some 200 years ago of the Bible Society, which has since distributed the Word of God throughout the world.

Before concluding this chapter, it is also important to note that Matthew, whose Gospel account was considered to be specifically addressed to a Jewish readership, regularly pointed out the various ways in which Jesus fulfilled Tanakh (Old Testament) prophecies about the Messiah. So at the end of the passage under consideration, when recording how Jesus healed all the sick and the demonised, Matthew explained that it was to fulfil the prophecy of Isaiah: *Surely he took up our pain and bore our suffering* (Matthew 8.17, quoting Isa 53.4).

Gentile Christians well versed in the Scriptures (sadly all too few in number in the West today) understand their great debt to the Jews; how God has called them to assist their return to the Holy Land, to pray for the peace of Jerusalem and to say to them (or remind them): *Your God reigns!* (see Isa 52.7). Many today, including one of my friends, are engaged in helping Jews (often still under persecution in the diaspora) to make 'Aliyah' (Jewish immigration) by returning to their ancient homeland.

It also explains the actions of President Trump who, whatever you might think of him, has surrounded himself with dedicated pro-Israel Christians, who have wisely advised him to break the mould of political correctness, which will never bring peace to the Middle East, and recognise – at last – that Jerusalem is Israel's eternal capital.

But God knows, and we know, who will usher in that peace – the One referred to by Isaiah as *Shar Shalom*, the Prince of Peace (see Isa 9.6).

Israel – and Jewish people everywhere – will continue to be troubled by the devil and his henchmen, but they can rest assured that they will be blessed and supported by those who truly love the God of Israel, whom Christians believe is the Father of Jesus, the Messiah.

When wise men from the east came to worship the new-born Christ, they asked, *Where is the one who has been born king of the Jews? We saw his star when it rose and have come to worship him* (Matthew 2.2). The wise men, or Magi, are generally reputed to have been from the same priestly sect of the Persian royal court that had once included the prophet Daniel. They were also quite likely to have been Jews (not Gentiles) as the Persian Diaspora was estimated to number tens of thousands at the time of Jesus. They were not only keen astronomers, but also clearly well versed in the Jewish Scriptures. In following the star to Bethlehem, their journey could well have coincided with one of the Jewish feasts – quite possibly Tabernacles, when we are reminded of how God chooses to live among us. And it is not surprising that, a generation later, Jews from Persia (Parthians, Medes and Elamites) were present on the Day of Pentecost (Acts 2.9).[2]

It is also worth pointing out that one of the much-loved carols sung around the world each Christmas – *The First Nowell*[3] – focuses on the worship of the new-born Messiah by the shepherds and the wise men and contains the memorable refrain, "Noel, Noel, Noel, Noel, born is the King of Israel". More than 2,000 years later, even global music icon Kanye West has nailed his colours to the mast with his new album *Jesus is King*.

Theologian Frank Booth sheds further light on the gifts the wise men brought: "Sources outside the Bible attest that

Persian Diaspora Jews still brought tribute to the Temple during the first century AD. Such tribute would quite likely have comprised small high-value commodities like gold as well as spices from the east such as incense and myrrh, which were not only stock-in-trade for quality goods regularly brought into the empire from eastern merchants on their camel trains, but would also have been readily acceptable, indeed highly valued, for Temple worship. It would have been easy to pack a bit extra as gifts for the baby, if they could find him."

When Jesus stood trial, the high priest asked him if he was the Jewish Messiah, the Son of God (see Matthew 26.63f). The Roman governor, Pontius Pilate, then asked him if he was indeed the King of the Jews (see Matthew 27.11). The answer to both questions was a clear: *You have said so*. The charge (of alleged blasphemy) against him written above his head as he died in agony on the cross thus read: *THIS IS JESUS, THE KING OF THE JEWS* (See Matthew 27.37.) But the chief priests were not happy with this. They wanted it to record that *this man claimed to be king of the Jews* (John 19.21). But Pilate famously answered: *What I have written, I have written* (John 19.22).

As a descendant of Jews who have blessed the Gentiles, and as a Gentile who has been blessed by the Jews, and those who love them, may I commend to you... Jesus, long-awaited Jewish Messiah and Saviour of the world!

[1] The Talmud (the Jewish commentary on the Bible) pictures the Messiah as carefully bandaging the wounds of lepers, instead of shunning them. It also seems that Jesus fulfilled the purity laws, which forbid contact with people afflicted by skin diseases.
[2] My thanks to Frank Booth for digging out these valuable nuggets of information.
[3] Or Nowell, an ancient spelling of Noel, an alternative word for Christmas.

CHAPTER 2 – JESUS IN THE TANAKH

Not long ago, after a talk at the clubhouse premises of my old church – All Souls, Langham Place, in central London – I was challenged to explain what I meant by saying that Israeli Prime Minister Benjamin Netanyahu was a Bible-believer, when he evidently was not a New Testament Christian. A good question, so I will attempt to answer it while also dealing with the whole question of Jesus in the Tanakh. We start in the New Testament where we read how the risen Jesus engaged with the two disciples (including Cleopas) on the road to Emmaus (already mentioned in the Introduction). They were glum and despondent and, although they had heard rumours of his resurrection, they were desperately disappointed – even depressed, perhaps. What did Jesus say to them? "It is all in the Scriptures" (meaning the Old Testament of course at that time) – Scriptures which were indeed inspired by God (2 Timothy 3.16) and authenticated by our Lord when he contested with the devil in the Wilderness. In fact, everything required for salvation in Jesus is in the Old Testament (2 Timothy 3.15)!

We see how (in Luke 24.32) he *opened the Scriptures* to them. Jewish people (and others too) are well able to find their Messiah in the Tanakh! I remember a Norwegian girl from my days at All Souls who, in her search for God, began reading the Bible from the very beginning and was converted by the time she got to Numbers – only the fourth of its 66 books, still part of the Torah, the five books of Moses. This is what Jesus is referring to here on the road to Emmaus. Come, let us travel further along that golden highway.

In v.26 of the above-mentioned passage, Jesus refers to how the Scriptures say he will have to *suffer these things* before entering into his glory. He was no doubt thinking, for example, of Abraham being prepared to sacrifice his beloved son in obedience to the Lord. But at the last minute God intervenes by providing a ram caught by its horns in a thicket. Abraham called that place Moriah – *the Lord will provide*. And to this day it is said, *On the mountain of the Lord it will be provided* (Genesis 22.14). And indeed, from John 3.16, we see that *God so loved the world that he gave his only Son that whoever believes in him shall not die, but have eternal life*. Jesus was our perfect provision, the Lamb of God who died as a sacrifice for our sins. Indeed, Abraham, and all nations, were forever blessed because of that amazing act of obedience on Mt Moriah (proving that obedience is better than sacrifice: 1 Sam 15.22). But Abraham's act was a foretaste of a greater sacrifice in the very same vicinity when Jesus was obedient even unto death (Phil 2.8).

There is another New Testament passage which wonderfully bears out the truth of Jesus in the Tanakh; and it is at the other end of his earthly ministry – i.e. at the beginning, at the calling of the first disciples. John the Baptist hails him as the Lamb of God, as a result of which he loses two disciples to Jesus. One of them was Andrew, and the first thing he did was to find his brother Simon (Peter) and tell him: *We have found the Messiah*.

The next day, in Galilee, Philip joined Jesus, and he in turn found Nathanael and told him: *We have found the one Moses wrote about in the Law, and about whom the prophets also wrote – Jesus of Nazareth, the son of Joseph* (John 1.43-51, fulfilling Deut 18.15). Nathanael, in turn, wins high praise from the Lord – even at the very start of his discipleship: *Here truly is an Israelite in whom there is no deceit*. And when Nathanael realised that Jesus already knew him by divine revelation, he declared: *Rabbi, you are the Son of God; you are the king of Israel.* It seemed he got to this point well ahead of Peter. Jesus then tells Nathanael that he will see even greater things, referencing Jacob's dream of a stairway to heaven, implying that He is now the fulfilment of that dream.

Jesus was of course also a fulfilment of the Passover, when Jews celebrate their mighty deliverance from slavery in Egypt. Like the Messiah to come, Moses too was rescued from a slaughter of innocents just as Jesus would be. Remember how Pharaoh ordered the murder of all Hebrew boys, but the baby Moses was saved. And how King Herod ordered the murder of all baby boys in Bethlehem, but Jesus' parents were already safely in Egypt, having been warned by an angel to flee there. With judgment about to fall on the firstborn of Egypt, the Jews are instructed to daub the lintels and doorframes of their houses with the blood of a sacrificed lamb. And the Lord says, *When I see the blood, I will pass over you* (Ex 12.12f). This was a perfect picture of what was to happen at Calvary some 1,500 years later. The blood of the Lamb of God himself would be poured out on the wooden stakes cut down to nail Jesus to the cross, and all who trust in Him would be rescued from slavery to sin and death. The Lord would say of them: When I see the blood...Deborah, Sam, Miriam, Jacob...I will pass over you (and spare you from destruction of the wicked).

The Israelites were thus released, only for Pharaoh to change his mind and chase them all the way to the sea, where they found themselves hemmed in on all sides, with nowhere to flee – just as they are today in some respects, surrounded by implacable enemies determined to destroy them. But just at the point where they have nowhere to run, when there is no human hope, they have a Saviour who comes to their rescue. Moses stretched out his hand, the sea opened up and the Israelites crossed over on dry ground (Ex 14.21f). Jesus also stretched out his hands on the cross, enabling his people to cross over from death to life. The Red Sea crossing is what is depicted in baptism. The Jews would of course have drowned were it not for their Messiah who, through Moses, opened up the way. In the same way we identify with Jesus in his burial and resurrection (Col 2.12) when we go through the waters of baptism (*baptizo* is the Greek word for immerse).

Once rescued from death, we learn how to live our lives in God's way. The 40 years in the Wilderness was no picnic; it was a time of testing and training for God's people when they would learn that *man does not live on bread alone, but on every word that proceeds from the mouth of God* (see Deut 8.3; Matthew 4.4). They did not just need bread to eat and water to drink, but spiritual food to enable them to live lives of righteousness before God and their neighbours. Nevertheless, their bread to eat was a picture of the Messiah to come. For their daily manna was literally *bread from heaven* (Ex 16.4), a foretaste of He who was to come who identified himself as the *Bread of Life* (John 6.35). It was not just that he had fed the five thousand with five loaves and two fish, but *his* 'bread' would be supernatural food by which their spirits would be fed for eternity.

Remember, after his conversation with the Samaritan woman at Jacob's Well in Sychar, where he promised her *living water*, the disciples urged him to eat, but he replied: *I have food to eat that you know nothing about* and, *my food is to do the will of him who sent me and to finish his work* (John 4.32-34).

After feeding the crowds, Jesus warned them: *Do not work for food that spoils, but for food that endures to eternal life, which the Son of Man will give you* (John 6.27). And then he adds, dramatically, *I am the bread that came down from heaven* (v.41).... *Your ancestors ate manna and died, but whoever feeds on this bread will live forever* (v.58) – he was actually teaching in the synagogue at Capernaum (v.59).

It is said that 'bread is the staff of life' – providing a very basic need for nourishment. Yet Jesus offers us a kind of bread to enable us to really live life to the full (see John 10.10), meeting every need. After all, the Hebrew word for bread – *lechem* – means far more than just a loaf; it is an idiom for all that is needed to sustain life. We can stop searching here, there and everywhere for meaning and purpose, fun and fulfilment, adventure and thrill-seeking highs. Jesus offers us all that. Remember, he is our Provider. And the more of his bread we feed on, the more meaningful and exciting our lives become. I commend to you Jesus, the living bread that came down from heaven, and brought heaven to earth.

Naturally, of course, the Israelites were not only hungry for food but also thirsty as they wandered through the dry and sweltering desert. God provided them with water from the Rock at Horeb (Ex 17.6). Jesus is that rock (see Matthew 7.24f; 16.18) and provides us with living water (John 4.10) which, when drunk, will enable us never to thirst for anything else but that *spring of water welling up to eternal life* (John 4.14). He will fully satisfy our spiritual hunger and thirst; in fact, we will be more than satisfied and constantly overwhelmed.

At Mt Sinai, God gives us the Ten Commandments, of which Jesus is the ultimate fulfilment (see Exodus 20; Matthew 5.17) enabling us, through the Holy Spirit, to have the Law written on our hearts. And through the Law we learn of God's uniqueness: *I am the Lord...you shall have no other gods besides me*. Jesus is God manifest in the flesh, absolutely unique and the only way to the Father: *I am the way, and the truth, and the life; no-one comes to the Father except through me* (John 14.6). And this uniqueness also applies to the community purporting to follow God (Deut 7.1f). There is no room for compromise, intermarriage or treaties with other religions (Ezra 10.2, 2 Cor 6.14). The same applies to the New Testament community – Jesus is unique, the God of Israel is unique and his people (*ecclesia*) are unique.

Jesus keeps appearing throughout the Psalms, especially in Psalm 22, vv 1, 7f & 18, speaking so clearly of his future suffering at Calvary: *My God, my God, why have you forsaken me? All who see me mock me… they divide my clothes among them and cast lots for my garment.*

The prophets, especially Isaiah, give us many wonderful glimpses of the Messiah to come. Matthew's Gospel, which I also like to refer to as the gospel of Isaiah, includes many references to the prophet's predictions. Here is one: *Therefore the Lord himself will give you a sign: the virgin will conceive and give birth to a son, and will call him Immanuel.* (Isa 7.14) Here is another: *…in the future he will honour Galilee of the nations… the people walking in darkness have seen a great light…for unto us a child is born, to us a son is given, and the government will be on his shoulders. And he will be called Wonderful Counsellor, Mighty God, Everlasting Father, Prince of Peace* (Isa 9.1-6). And from Micah 5.2: *But you, Bethlehem Ephrathah, though you are small among the clans of Judah, out of you will come for me one who will be ruler over Israel, whose origins are from of old, from ancient times.*

Back to Isaiah, where chapter 52.7 describes: *How beautiful on the mountains are the feet of those who bring good news…* I have seen this in one sense as a call to Gentiles like me to proclaim the gospel of salvation, but after visiting the mountain where Jesus is said to have preached the most famous message ever, it speaks also to me of He whose beautiful feet in ancient times did walk the shores of Galilee and proclaim from that blessed mount above it the good news that would forever change the world. Jesus is the ultimate bringer of good news. But, as we learn from just a few verses later, it is the bad news first. As Jesus told the disciples on the Emmaus road: *Did not the Messiah have to suffer these things and then enter his glory?... He was despised and rejected of men, a man of sorrows and familiar with grief... but he was pierced for our transgressions...* and: *after he has suffered, he will see the light of life and be satisfied...* (Isa 53.3, 5, 11).

And so, not long after these very Scriptures were fulfilled, a godly and high-ranking Ethiopian official was travelling in his chariot on the road from Jerusalem to Gaza, and he just happened to be reading this very portion of Isaiah. The Holy Spirit sent Philip the evangelist to explain it to him. *Then Philip began with that very passage of Scripture and told him the good news about Jesus* (see Acts 8.35). He was baptised straight away (no six-week course) and went on his way rejoicing, no doubt becoming the first ever missionary to Africa!

The gospel is also foretold very clearly in the little book of Jonah (1.17). The prophet was called to preach repentance in Nineveh, but was running away (or sailing away, more like) from his calling. (If God has called you, and you messed up, well, he is still calling you; so you have time to put it right – *for the gifts and calling of God are irrevocable* (see Romans 11.29). Anyway, he ended up being swallowed by a huge fish where he stayed for three days and three nights before he was spewed up alive on the beach. According to Matthew, the religious leaders were asking Jesus for a sign of his authority, to which he replied: *A wicked and adulterous generation asks for a sign! But none will be given it except the sign of the prophet Jonah. For as Jonah was three days and three nights in the belly of a huge fish, so the Son of Man will be three days and three nights in the heart of the earth* (Matthew 12.39f). They got their sign, but did they believe? Judging from the ensuing verses, and from what we know – apparently not. Nineveh repented, and the Queen of Sheba came from the ends of the earth to seek Solomon's wisdom – they would stand in judgment on this generation, said Jesus.

Then we have that mysterious character Melchizedek, first appearing in Genesis 14.18 almost out of nowhere. He was from of old, without beginning (Hebrews 7.3) and *brought out bread and wine*. He blessed Abraham, and he himself was blessed with what Abraham gave. He was surely a foreshadowing of the role of Messiah and, as King of Salem, of the centrality of Jerusalem in God's purposes. He only had a walk-on part in those early chapters of the Bible, but it was a crucial one. In the case of Christ, his earthly ministry lasted just three years, a tiny fraction of history, and yet it changed the world forever.

This reminds me of a meeting I once attended to consider (with the 2020 400th anniversary of the sailing of the Mayflower in mind) how the churches of our area (South Yorkshire, North Nottinghamshire) should celebrate the influence and impact of the Pilgrim Fathers, most of whom came from our region but who were hounded out of the country after making a stand for their biblical beliefs during the years 1606-1608. However, it was decided we should instead celebrate all Christians in the area who had made a lasting contribution to the faith. One of those present suggested it would be wrong to focus on a group whose contribution to our Christian heritage lasted only three years! Ugh!

In the event, they initially escaped to Holland before finally sailing for the New World – this time with the King's blessing – in 1620. And they went on to found what became the greatest nation on earth!

In the same way Jesus, whose appearance on earth, like Melchizedek's, was so brief, now deserves our full attention and adoring worship.

Job, through all his pain and torment, was able to say: *I know that my Redeemer lives, and that he will stand at the latter day upon the earth* (Job 19.25). He is looking prophetically at both the future resurrection and the Second Coming of our Lord who, according to the prophet Zechariah, would in later times, when the Middle East is shaken by terrible violence, place his feet on the Mt of Olives, echoing what the angels told the *men from Galilee* on that same mountain when the risen Saviour ascended to heaven: *This same Jesus, who has been taken from you into heaven, will come back in the same way you have seen him go into heaven* (Acts 1.11).

Zechariah also foretells of an extraordinary revival among the Jewish people in Israel around this time when Elohim would *pour out on the house of David and the inhabitants of Jerusalem a spirit of grace and supplication. They will look on me* [or to me]*, the one they have pierced, and they will mourn for him as one mourns for an only child....* And a fountain would be opened to cleanse them from sin and impurity (see Zech 12.10 & 13.1). Echoing this, the Apostle Paul speaks of a day when *all Israel will be saved* for, as he explains, they have *experienced a hardening in part until the full number of the Gentiles has come in* (Rom 11.25f).

This great and wondrous ingathering was foreshadowed in Egypt some 4,000 years ago when the patriarch Joseph, thrown into a well and sold into slavery by his jealous siblings, finally reveals himself to his brothers, who had come to benefit from his wisdom as Pharaoh's deputy in storing up grain for the famine which he himself had predicted.

Read Genesis 45.1-7: *Then Joseph could no longer control himself before all his attendants, and he cried out, Have everyone leave my presence! So there was no-one with Joseph when he made himself known to his brothers. And he wept so loudly that the Egyptians heard him, and Pharaoh's household heard about it. Joseph said to his brothers, I am Joseph! Is my father still living? But his brothers were not able to answer him, because they were terrified at his presence. Then Joseph said to his brothers, Come close to me. When they had done so, he said, I am your brother Joseph, the one you sold into Egypt! And now, do not be distressed and do not be angry with yourselves for selling me here, because it was to save lives that God sent me ahead of you. For two years now there has been famine in the land, and for the next five years there will be no ploughing and reaping. But God sent me ahead of you to preserve for you a remnant on earth and to save your lives by a great deliverance.*

In revealing himself to his brothers, he does so with Gentiles not present, to save their dignity and embarrassment. He weeps loudly for them. This is the moment for which he has been waiting for so long. The revelation of Yeshua to the Jewish people, his brothers, will be the climax of the ages, coinciding with his return and the setting up of his millennial reign of peace and triumph. Later, Joseph says: *You intended to harm me, but God intended it for good to accomplish what is now being done, the saving of many lives. So then, don't be afraid. I will provide for you and your children.* He reassured them and spoke kindly to them (see Gen 50.20f).

This is our Jesus, once again the Provider of Israel. He will reassure and speak kindly to his Jewish brothers when they recognise him as the one they have pierced, and say to them: You meant it for evil, but God meant it for good – so that countless lives all down the centuries could be saved for eternity through my death for their sins on the cross. If you had all recognised me for who I was, they would never have heard the gospel, because there would never have been a Lamb of God to take away the sins of the world.

So you see, it is all there – in the Tanakh. It all points to Jesus, as he told his friends on the road to Emmaus. And praise God for the New Testament, which completes the picture.

The famine which drew Joseph's brothers to Egypt is today a famine of God's authentic Word which will surely draw seeking Jews to the One who has become Saviour to much of the Gentile world. Pour out your Spirit on your people, O Lord! Amen.

CHAPTER 3 – DEAD SEA COMES TO LIFE!

At the end of 2018 I was studying the Book of Ezekiel in preparation for a weekend retreat when a friend forwarded me a YouTube clip announcing the most incredible news, which is surely another significant sign of the imminent return of Jesus.

One of Ezekiel's famous prophecies – widely thought to be allegorical rather than literal – was now being fulfilled just as he said it would 2,600 years ago!

In short, the Dead Sea is coming alive! Yes, fresh water is now reported to be flowing into this Rift Valley expanse that has been unable to support life since the destruction of Sodom and Gomorrah thousands of years ago, useful only for drawing tourists to sample its healing properties while floating unsupported. Freshwater fish have been seen swimming in the surrounding sinkholes that have opened up in recent years as the sea, made up of 33% salt, has been receding. See *CBN News* clip at https://youtu.be/XzXw3fGP2Tw In chapter 47 of Ezekiel, who prophesied while in exile in Babylon from 597 BC, the prophet describes a vision of an increasingly deep river flowing from the Temple in Jerusalem down towards the Dead Sea, bringing new life wherever it flows and supporting the same kind of fish as those inhabiting the Mediterranean.

Ezekiel wrote: *He said to me: This water flows towards the eastern region and goes down into the Arabah (the Jordan Valley), where it enters the Sea (the Dead Sea). When it empties into the Sea, the water there becomes fresh. Swarms of living creatures will live wherever the river flows. There will be large numbers of fish, because this water flows there*

*and makes the salt water fresh; so where the river flows
everything will live. Fishermen will stand along the shore;
from En Gedi to En Eglaim there will be places for spreading
nets. The fish will be of many kinds, like the fish of the Great
Sea (the Mediterranean)* (Ezek 47.8-10).

The vision comes amid the latter part of the book dealing
with the promised restoration of the Jewish people both to
their land and their Lord. And I believe the 'resurrection'
of a dead stretch of water reflects a time (near the end of
the age) when the fortunes of Israel – long forsaken and
persecuted – would be turned around.

This is what the world is now witnessing with the Jewish
state emerging as a major player on the global scene with
a thriving economy borne out of extraordinary innovation.
At the same time there is a growing movement among Jews
acknowledging that Jesus is the long-promised Messiah,
fulfilling the word that when they are finally restored from
all the nations to which they were dispersed because of
forsaking God's ways, they would be given a 'new heart'
and, as with the Dead Sea, cleansed and 'sprinkled clean'
of their sins (see Ezek 36.24-26).

Ezekiel mirrors the New Testament Gospels in so many
ways. It would seem he plays the Elijah/John the Baptist role
in the opening half, calling Israel to repent of her detestable
idolatries and warning of great disaster to come with the total
destruction of Jerusalem by the Babylonians.

In this and other ways he can also be seen as a forerunner
of Christ. For example, the Lord keeps addressing him as
'son of man', a title Jesus adopted for himself. Like Jesus
too, he predicted the downfall of the holy city, and both
prophecies were precisely fulfilled – by the Babylonians
in Ezekiel's day and by the Romans within a generation of
our Lord's warning.

Another intriguing parallel with Jesus is that Ezekiel

began prophesying at the age of 30 when he would normally have become priest (he was in the priestly line of Zadok) – except that there was no Temple in Babylon. And we know that this was the same age[1] that Christ – prophet, priest and King – began a ministry that was to last just three years, the equivalent length of Ezekiel's early prophecies warning the Israelites of the disastrous consequences of their godless behaviour.

But few people then, as now, want to hear the truth. They would rather hear words of 'peace, peace' when there is, in reality, no peace (see Ezek 13.10, Jer 6.14).

But while he was in exile among those paying the price of their waywardness, Ezekiel announces good news of future restoration when they will be back in the "land flowing with milk and honey" and their sins will be paid for.

This section seems to speak not only of their return from Babylon, but also of a future return after a much more widespread dispersion judging from the references to "all the countries" to which they have been scattered.

They would not only be back in the land on this later occasion, but also enjoying a renewed relationship with the Lord who will give them a heart of flesh instead of a heart of stone along with the ability to follow his decrees wholeheartedly. There is even talk of being circumcised in "heart and flesh", pre-empting the New Testament emphasis on true circumcision – that of the heart.

In fact, judgment between the sheep and the goats – later elaborated upon by Jesus in Matthew 25.31-46 – is dealt with as part of the section on Israel's restoration (see Ezek 34.17). The implication is that recognition of God's hand on his people would separate one member of the flock from another, especially as far as nations are concerned.

Ezekiel's vision of the Valley of Dry Bones follows immediately after this good news; and in the eyes of many, including long-serving Israeli Prime Minister Binyamin Netanyahu, it is seen as a picture of the nation of Israel rising out of the ashes of the Holocaust, effectively coming back to life through the breath (or Spirit) of God.

In this respect, it is not widely known that there were an estimated 100,000 Jewish believers in Jesus by 1939 thanks to the work of missions such as CMJ (the Church's Ministry among Jewish people). So the process of spiritual redemption had already begun when all the hordes of hell tried to prevent its completion, and the inevitable return of their Messiah that would follow.

Nevertheless, since the rebirth of the Jewish state – and especially since the 1967 reunification of Jerusalem – the Messianic Jewish movement has seen vital growth.

The prophet then looks even further into the future with prophecies also reflected in the Book of Revelation, describing how nations led by Gog and Magog (possibly Russia and its allies, Iran in particular) will come from the north with a great army against Jerusalem. But the Lord will meet them with fire and sulphur – a flashback perhaps to Sodom's demise while also indicating the possible use of nuclear weapons.

Israelis would spend seven months burying the enemy dead as God displays his power and glory, and especially his love for his chosen ones. And it is in this context I believe that all Jewish people would finally be gathered to Israel – *not leaving any behind* (Ezek 39.28).

Perhaps this is also the time when *all Israel will be saved* (Romans 11.26), judging from the ensuing verse: *I will no longer hide my face from them, for I will pour out my Spirit on the house of Israel, declares the Sovereign Lord* (v29) – also reminiscent of Joseph revealing himself to his brothers.

It is not widely known that the very first line of the Lord's Prayer – *Hallowed by thy name,* or, *may your name be sanctified* in more modern versions – is a plea for the return of the Jewish exiles as much as it is for a general hallowing of his name. As my friend and theologian Dr Fred Wright points out, there is only one Scripture that explains how the Lord's name may thus be hallowed, or sanctified, and it is found in a passage from Ezekiel chapter 36 (beginning at verse 16) that, in the Hebrew Bible, is headed *Kidush ha Shem* (The Sanctification of God's Holy Name).

Jewish exile is a consequence of their rebellion against God whose holy name is constantly profaned while they remain in foreign lands, *for it was said of them, These are the Lord's people, and yet they had to leave his land* (v20). So it is out of concern for his holy name, which they have profaned (a word used five times in this short passage) by their exile, that the Lord will bring them back (see vv24-26).

The numerous benefits of their return – quite apart from God's reputation – are subsequently listed, and they include a plentiful harvest reaped by a people with a new spirit, set apart once more to walk the way of holiness with their God. And so, although the modern nation state of Israel may be seen by many (including Christians) as an irrelevant political issue to be avoided, it is in fact the complete opposite. It is the greatest sign of our times for which we should be praying every day.

Ezekiel goes on to include an extraordinarily detailed description of a vast (presumably third) Temple obviously yet to be built as the Second Temple was much more modest. Many Christians object to such a thought on the grounds that in Christ we are the temple of the Holy Spirit. But if it is in Scripture, and all prophecy so far fulfilled has come to pass precisely as predicted, then we should surely wait and see. Besides, work on a Third Temple is going on behind the scenes as I write. In fact, preparations are reported to be in full swing. For example, the breeding of the traditional red heifer is now complete.

According to *Israel Today*, "the Temple Institute already houses the three most important items for the new Temple, which have been manufactured precisely in accordance with the biblical specifications: the golden altar of incense, showbread table and the Temple menorah made of 24-carat gold."[2]

It does also seem to be part and parcel of the New Jerusalem depicted in Revelation with gates named after the twelve tribes of Israel. But as we have seen, a very significant aspect of these temple chapters is being fulfilled in a remarkable way right now with fresh water reported to be flowing into the Dead Sea, supporting marine life it has not seen for thousands of years since the destruction of Sodom and Gomorrah on its shores with fire and brimstone.

That terrible judgment came about because of gross sin among its people – particularly pride and arrogance, and what became known as sodomy (homosex sin). And although God will still judge the wicked today – he has not changed his mind about sin – we are nevertheless living in a period of mercy when God is giving maximum opportunity for people (especially Israel, his 'treasured possession') to repent of their selfish ways and turn back to him.

Do I take any pleasure in the death of the wicked? declares the Sovereign Lord. Rather, am I not pleased when they turn from their ways and live? (Ezek 18.23).

God records with disgust (1 Sam 8.5) how Israel wanted to be like other nations in their idolatry and even in sacrificing their children in the fire. But when his chosen ones are back in the land he promised them so long ago, they will know that God has done it – and indeed today he is pouring out his blessing upon them: the hills are dripping with wine and the fields are filling the world with fruit, just as the prophets foretold (Isa 27.6), while the nation has emerged as one of the world's strongest economies leading the way in many areas of technology and innovation.

And now even the Dead Sea is coming to life in fulfilment of a 2,600-year-old prophecy! You can be sure that all prophecy of Scripture will be fulfilled to the letter.

Around three-quarters of Ezekiel's predictions (81% of Bible prophecies on the whole) have already been fulfilled with pinpoint accuracy.[3] Take, for example, his prophecy of Tyre's downfall. He said the Eastern Mediterranean fishing port would one day be razed to the ground and thrown into the sea, and the bare rock where it once stood would become a place for fishermen to dry their nets.

No other city, before or since, has ever been thrown into the sea, writes author and Bible teacher David Pawson in his masterful work *Unlocking the Bible*. "When Alexander the Great came marching down towards Egypt with his great army, the people of Tyre simply got into their fishing boats and sailed to the island half-a-mile offshore, knowing that Alexander had an army but not a navy."[4]

But when Alexander saw this (he wasn't called Great for nothing), he commanded that every brick, every stone and every piece of timber in the city be used to build a causeway to the island, after which his army went across and defeated the people of Tyre.

Even today, fishermen's nets are spread out on the bare rock of old Tyre, just as Ezekiel prophesied, while the modern city is out on the island with sand having silted up against Alexander's causeway. If it's in the Bible, you had better believe it!

Ezekiel has also profoundly affected my own personal life in two specific ways. The first relates to a time way back in 1980 when I answered a call to "stand in the gap" as a watchman for the Lord (warning people of the consequences of sin and godlessness) at the Full Gospel Business Men's

Fellowship International (FGBMFI) European Convention at Wembley Arena. The preacher's message was based on a passage from Ezekiel in which God laments the absence of anyone to 'stand in the gap' in this way (see Ezek 22.30).

The other, more recent, way in which the prophet was especially used in my life came about in the year 2000 when a verse from chapter 9 confirmed to my then new girlfriend Linda that she should marry me! I was widowed at the time and she had asked the Lord for assurance as to whether I was the right choice for her life's partner, and he subsequently spoke to her heart directly from a rather obscure verse which told of *a man clothed in linen who had a writing kit at his side* (Ezek 9.2).

The Lord then said to her: "I want you to support the man with the writing kit!" And of course I am forever grateful for that. I could not believe the extraordinary change in her demeanour towards me when I next called at her home. She had heard from the Lord – and that changed everything!

But we can all be assured that God is returning to his holy city because the end of this prophetic book actually tells us that it will be named *The Lord is there* (Ezek 48.35).

A river of life from God's throne is also depicted on the last page of the Bible in the Book of Revelation, which is all about what will happen in the days immediately preceding the Second Coming of Christ.

The biblical symbolism of life from the dead relates both to Israel (see Romans 11.15) and their Messiah. We are living in momentous times that could well usher in the return of our Lord. Watch and pray so that you (and your loved ones) are not caught unawares.

[1] A male adult would not have been allowed to speak in public until he was 30.
[2] *Israel Today* magazine, November 2018
[3] *Unlocking the Bible*, David Pawson
[4] Ibid.

CHAPTER 4 – TOTAL INTEGRITY

A study of Nathanael – John 1.43-51

Nothing to hide, nothing to declare and nothing to do... Sounds like someone ready to go on an adventurous journey of discovery. Well, it is; and it could apply to you too. Nathanael was one of Jesus' first disciples and evidently an amazing character, yet little heralded in the Scriptures. He only plays a walk-on part; a short passage in chapter 1 of John's Gospel along with a brief mention at 21.2 which tells us he is from Cana in Galilee, but what a star he is. For if the potential he showed at the initial stage of his discipleship is anything to go by, he will no doubt have become a major player of the New Testament era.

He may not have become one of the Twelve Apostles (though he has often been identified with Bartholomew, mentioned in the synoptic Gospels and Acts 1.13), but he was nevertheless the first disciple to recognise who Jesus was, proclaiming him *the Son of God, the King of Israel*. If you conducted a survey of Christians, I suggest many would say that it was Peter, which is understandable because his confession is so well known and comes at the time Jesus challenges his followers as to who they believe he is – but that came much later in his ministry. (On the other hand, you could say John the Baptist was the first to recognise his divinity, but he was a prophet in his own right pointing his own disciples to Jesus as the 'Lamb of God'.) Nathanael's confession, however, takes place immediately after the incident with John the Baptist, at the very start of our Lord's miraculous ministry, and the divine revelation of his whereabouts – under the fig tree – was perhaps the first fruit of the miracles to come.

But I do not want to focus on Nathanael's revelation of Jesus as Messiah. I am more intrigued with the Lord's lofty commendation of him as *an Israelite in whom there is no deceit (or guile)*. Wow! Surely one of the highest accolades God gives to any character in the Bible. We remember how David was declared to be *a man after God's own heart*, but this too surely ranks high in the charts.

Here is a man who is transparently honest and truthful. He says exactly what he thinks; he says precisely what is on his mind – no sham, no deception or cover-up or secret thoughts. (We have a delightful teenage nephew and godson like that; and his name is also Nathaniel – with a different spelling – for whom we have high hopes). Perhaps the New Testament Nathanael is also a little sceptical, judging from his question to Philip, who wants him to meet *the one Moses wrote about in the Law, and about whom the prophets also wrote – Jesus of Nazareth, the son of Joseph.*

Nathanael asks his friend: *Nazareth! Can anything good come from there?* Philip doesn't tell him off for his scepticism, or for bad-mouthing the Galilean town where Jesus grew up, which is hardly surprising as it was considered a hotbed for non-observant, Romanised Jews. No, he simply says: *Come and see.* And he was willing to check out Jesus' credentials; he needed confirmation of the claims for his Messiahship. He was willing to *taste and see that the Lord is good* and that *good* could indeed come from Nazareth! If you seek, you will find. If you taste what God has for you, you will see that it is good.

Then, when Jesus saw Nathanael approaching, he said of him: *Here truly is an Israelite in whom there is no deceit.* The next part of the conversation is very revealing. Nathanael asks: *How do you know me?*

He recognises Jesus' description of his character. After all, he would not have been a man of integrity without knowing it. It would have been something he had worked on over the years, seeking to live by God's principles of honesty and truth liberally strewn throughout the Scriptures. How do I know that? Because it was clear that he was familiar with the Law of Moses, which we deduce from what Philip told him: *We have found the one Moses wrote about....* He had no doubt put the precepts of the law into practice as best as he knew how, and would have been very conscious of the necessity in God's world for speaking the truth, keeping his word and meaning what he said.

But it was only when he asked, *How do you know me?* that Jesus gives further confirmation of who he is with the divine revelation that he saw him under the fig tree: *I saw you while you were still under the fig tree before Philip called you.*

This must have been quite a shock as it would seem from the nature of the conversation that there was no way he could have known that from a human perspective. So he makes his staggering declaration: *Rabbi, you are the Son of God; you are the King of Israel.*

Notice how Jesus does not commend him as much for his declaration of faith as for his transparency – his total integrity. This is not because faith is less important – in fact it is vital; for without faith it is impossible to please God (Heb 11.6). But he was supernaturally helped to this position – Jesus helped him along by demonstrating a knowledge of him that only an all-seeing God could have. He actually mildly rebukes him, saying *You believe (or Do you believe?) because I told you I saw you under the fig tree. You will see greater things than that.*

Jesus then addressed them both (the Greek for *you* here is plural), hinting at his miraculous ministry to come by referring to the account of Jacob's stairway to heaven dream: *You will see heaven open, and the angels of God ascending and descending on the Son of Man.*

Indeed, they were about to witness the amazing miracles recorded in the Gospels – how Jesus turned water into wine, and walked on water, the feeding of the 5,000, the healing of the blind, the lame and the leper, and the raising of the dead. It would be the fulfilment, as it were, of Jacob's dream (Genesis 28.12) when the Lord told the son of Isaac how his descendants would inherit the land and be a blessing to all the peoples of the earth. Now Jesus is preaching good news to the poor, and the nations are still being blessed through Abraham, Isaac and Jacob.

Well, I mentioned it at the start of this chapter, and it seemed to sum up the great opportunity set before Nathanael – *Nothing to hide, nothing to declare, nothing to do*. He had nothing to hide; he was transparently truthful. He had nothing to declare (no contraband or dodgy baggage he wanted to slip through customs) and he had nothing to do. Well, I do not know that for sure, but it certainly seemed he was not doing anything under the fig tree, except perhaps enjoying the shade from the hot sun (it gets very hot in Galilee), or perhaps picking some fruit because he was hungry. Or just taking a rest. The thing is, he clearly did not have anything urgent on his schedule to distract him from seeking the Lord whom his friend was suggesting was the Messiah. He was ready to go, ready for take-off, perfectly placed to board the great journey of adventure in being a disciple of Jesus. He was ready, as the writer to the Hebrews put it, to *throw off everything that hinders and the sin that so easily entangles* so he could *run with perseverance the race marked out* for him (see Hebrews 12.1).

There is also heavy symbolism in Nathanael's first meeting with Jesus. He is sitting under a fig tree (which is widely seen as the biblical symbol of Israel, the nation, God's chosen people), clearly significant or it would not have been mentioned. Bearing in mind Jesus' reference to Jacob's dream in this context, are we here seeing a reversal of the deceit which had so characterised the son of Isaac before his encounters with God, first at Bethel and later at Peniel where, after the blessing he received following his famous struggle with God, he was re-named Israel? (See Gen 32.22-32, Hosea 12.4.)

Jacob had a bad start as the deceiver who tricked his father into giving him the blessing of the first-born meant for his older twin Esau, but he was abundantly fruitful in the end thanks to a testimony of transformation, including the wonderful reconciliation with his brother.

By contrast Nathanael, in whom there was no deceit, had made a good start, and there was nothing – no character deficiency – to hold him back. He represented a new day of truth – as a disciple of the One who is *the Truth* – when falsehood would give way to the glory of the gospel that is good news for the poor.

There was a sense in which Nathanael, a man in whom there was no deceit, was now part of an ancient wrong being put right. This was how God meant his people to be. Jesus is the second Adam righting Adam's wrong in disobeying the command of God. As Isaiah foretold: *Though your sins are like scarlet, they shall be as white as snow* (Isa 1.18). Jesus washes us clean and writes his laws on our heart.

So as Jacob becomes Israel after wrestling with God and overcoming (see Genesis 32.24), Nathanael emerges as an Israelite in whom there is no deceit. But as with Jacob, he too needed a personal encounter with God. Integrity on its own was not enough, even though it came from 'loving the law' (Psalm 119.47 – *for I delight in your commands, because I love them*; see also Psalm 19.7-14). The patriarch not only experienced Bethel (the house of God) but also Peniel (the face of God).

We will practice truth when we meet *the* Truth! One of the greatest needs of our age is for a resurgence of honesty and truth instead of lies and propaganda; integrity that will not compromise.

Jeremiah spoke of God's heart when he wrote: *Go up and down the streets of Jerusalem, look around and consider, search through her squares. If you can find but one person who deals honestly and seeks the truth, I will forgive this city* (Jer 5.1).

Likewise, Isaiah's words also mirror the state of our nation: *No-one calls for justice; no-one pleads a case with integrity. They rely on empty arguments, they utter lies; they conceive trouble and give birth to evil.*

*So justice is driven back, and righteousness stands at a distance; truth has stumbled in the streets, honesty cannot enter. Truth is nowhere to be found, and whoever shuns evil becomes a prey (*Isa 59.4,14f).

Enough is enough. It has got to stop. To use the title of a gigantic prayer meeting in Pretoria, South Africa, *It's Time* to call for a resurgence of truth in our land. But judgment starts with the house of God, so we need to begin with our own hearts in order to lead the way for a revival of God's law.

Total integrity – that is the calling of true Christians!

CHAPTER 5 – THE JOY OF JOB

After taking a closer look at Ezekiel, I felt led to tackle Job, one of the most ancient Bible narratives addressing a hugely difficult subject – suffering – and generally considered among the hardest to understand. Anticipating misery, doom and gloom, I was knocked out by the extraordinarily upbeat nature of this book.

It is actually a story of thrilling triumph over dreadful adversity, and of maintaining trust and integrity through it all, offering both great literature and supreme wisdom as it ponders the big questions of life, especially: 'Why do good people suffer?'

Job was God's star example of a righteous man, foreshadowing the agonies of the Christ to come, who had to suffer to serve the divine purpose. Jesus was God's beloved Son, in whom he was well pleased; Job was his choice of a man who steadfastly obeyed his commands. He was immensely proud of him, which is why he boasted to Satan: *Have you considered my servant Job?* (Job 1.8).

But Satan suggested he was only serving him faithfully because he was so blessed. So he allowed Satan to test him – and it was a very severe trial indeed, but he came through as gold refined by fire, maintaining his trust to the end, and was able to say: *Though he slay me, yet will I hope in him* (Job 13.15).

Satan is the accuser of the brethren (Rev 12.10, Zech 3.1), the counsel for the prosecution if you like. But he can only go so far. In the same way that God allowed him to test Job, he also permitted him to bring about Jesus' death on the cross, with even his own Son asking the question, *Why?*

(See Matthew 27.46, Psalm 22.1).

Job had many complaints, or questions, about why he was apparently suffering unjustly despite his commitment to God's Law, but his lack of understanding never amounted to a denial of his faith. His reward was a double portion like Elisha, so that the latter part of his life was more blessed and prosperous than the first.

If the 'prosperity gospel' was based on Job's testimony, then it is best fulfilled by a life of great suffering, mirrored by Jesus' own example. Prosperity *is* a reward for faithfulness, but that comes through thick and thin, through heights and depths, water and fire – even a fiery furnace.

In Isaiah's passage of the suffering Servant, he writes that *the will of the Lord will prosper in his hand. After the suffering of his soul, he will see the light of life and be satisfied* (Isa 53.10f).

Job's experience – like the Messiah's too of course – was also a portent of what Israel would go through as a nation during the Holocaust, yet out of this terrible torment would emerge vibrant new life, even a resurrection, along with ransom, redemption and restoration.

People talk of having the 'patience of Job', but that did not mean he never complained, argued with God or asked questions about why his efforts to please his Maker had evidently incurred trouble and strife. Were such efforts in vain? That was his dilemma. But he was determined never to forsake God no matter what.

The description of people as *Job's comforters* usually applies to those who offer superficial answers to life's troubles without having worn the shoes or trod the path of those they are trying to help. We can only truly empathise with those who are suffering if we have walked the road they are travelling.

For anyone who has experienced the pain of divorce,

adultery or widowhood, only those who have gone through the same trauma can really understand their grief. But Jesus has truly tasted their pain – on the cross, where he bore our sins – and shares their suffering.

Though the advice of Job's friends is recorded in Scripture and actually contains much sound counsel, they do not necessarily express God's mind, as is evident from his criticism of them. They were sure Job must have been sinning to have incurred such disaster, while Job protests his innocence and is finally vindicated. His experience was clearly an exception to the rule that you reap what you sow.

They may not have understood his distressing dilemma, but did at times offer worthy suggestions, which we will look at.

The book includes a wonderful description of the leviathan (what we now assume to be a crocodile) and you almost wonder why it is there. Is he being taken on some kind of wildlife safari? No, he is being told in dramatic terms that God cannot be treated as a pet. He cannot be tamed. He is not someone you take for a walk, or exercise, at your own discretion – someone you keep on a lead for a companion to fend off loneliness or burglars. The Almighty will lash out with fury and judgment on the unrighteous, who will be devoured without mercy if they do not repent of their ungodly ways. He is not a God without teeth, which he will use to crush his opponents.

Overall, Job is a magnificent testimony of triumph over adversity and misunderstanding, in finding out the ways of God that are ultimately beyond understanding, but nevertheless full of perfect wisdom and deep compassion, as he knows the end from the beginning, and wants always to bring out the best in us, transforming hurtful circumstances to good outcomes in line with his will.

Like Nathanael (see John 1.47), Job was a man of total

integrity – honest about his doubts, suffering and complaints but ultimately holding on to God and the truth.

In many ways he was a type of Christ, a man of righteousness suffering injustice, mocked and spat at, a man of sorrows acquainted with grief (see Isaiah 53). And yet, as Jesus *for the joy set before him endured the cross* (Hebrews 12.2) looking to the salvation of men and his own resurrection, Job too experienced a kind of resurrection in that the latter part of his life was more blessed than the first. In fact, he received a double portion of prosperity. He knew God better than he did before, so that he was able to say: *My ears had heard of you but now my eyes have seen you* (Job 42.5).

Out of the ashes of loss and mourning came beauty and long life – another 140 years no less – so that *nowhere in all the land were there found women as beautiful as Job's daughters...* (42.15f). The clear implication is that his wife must have been a beautiful woman, not to say fertile – and there is something very special about having a beautiful daughter! I should know. Part of Messiah's role was *to comfort all who mourn* and *to bestow on them a crown of beauty instead of ashes* (Isaiah 61.2f).

A word about Job's wife. Her faith clearly did not match his, and she was hardly supportive, suggesting that he *Curse God and die!* Job rightly rebukes her, wisely adding: *Shall we accept good from God, and not trouble?* (2.9f.)

Satan grossly underestimated the character of Job. His contention was that he only feared God because of his immense wealth and large family. So he was given permission to remove these blessings, but spare his life. Job duly lost all his possessions and all ten of his children to a combination of raiding parties and natural disaster. But his extraordinary response was that he had come into the world naked, and would leave it in the same way, adding:

*The Lord gave and the Lord has taken away; may the name
of the Lord be praised* (Job 1.21).

I think of the 19th century hymn-writer Horatio Spafford
who, after losing all four of his daughters when their ship
sank during an Atlantic crossing, was able to pen these
wondrous words: "When peace like a river attendeth my
way, when sorrow like sea billows roll, whatever my lot thou
hast taught me to say; it is well, it is well, with my soul!"

A lawyer by profession, Horatio had sent his family ahead
of him while he sorted out business matters in his native
Chicago. His wife was saved in the tragedy (as with Job), and
they had more children, finally settling in Jerusalem, where
they helped to found the so-called American Colony and
engaged in philanthropic work among the city's residents.

Though Job certainly questioned why he was having to
suffer so, he did not sin "by charging God with wrongdoing"
(Job 1.22). As if this was not enough of a test, Job was then
afflicted with painful sores all over his body.

Three friends came to console him, and apparently did
their best, offering wisdom and insight worthy of being
included in Scripture, but ultimately they were unable truly
to empathise because, obviously, they were not in his shoes.
Nor had they worn his shoes.

Having said that, they did the right thing by mourning with
those who mourn (see Rom 12.15), but sat in silence for an
entire week, not knowing what to say, a common affliction
for those of us seeking to comfort others in their trouble
(see 2.12f). We are embarrassed by people's suffering; yet
breaking the silence can be unhelpful and must be borne on
wisdom's wings.

If there was a flaw in Job's character, it was perhaps his
statement admitting *What I feared (*literally *feared most) has
come upon me; what I dreaded has happened to me* (3.25).
It is not a healthy spiritual trait to fear the worst or dwell

upon disasters that may befall us. We are called to live by faith, trusting God that he can turn whatever happens to us both to his and our advantage (see Romans 8.28). *For he wounds, but he also binds up; he injures, but his hands also heal* (5.18).

In anticipating his demise, Job says: *You will look for me, but I will be no more* (7.8) – a statement almost identical to that made by Jesus in confronting his opponents: *You will look for me, but you will not find me…* (John 7.34).

Job does not have the same assurance about his future, but he prefigures the Messiah's message of everlasting life for his disciples, to whom he assured: *In a little while you will see me no more, and then after a little while you will see me* (John 16.16).

As Job further contemplates why he has been targeted for such trouble, he asks God: *What is man that you make so much of him…?* (7.17). It is a question echoed in Psalm 8.4: *What is man that you are mindful of him?* Why so much attention, care, interest, testing and constant desire for companionship? You can feel his frustration rising: *Will you never… let me alone even for an instant?* (7.19.)

God loves us so much, he cannot take his eyes off us; he watches our every move – not to trip us up, but with the hope of guiding and counselling us if only we should seek and embrace his advice. He is our potential bridegroom if only we would welcome his wooing and betroth ourselves to an eternal partnership with him.

Bildad, Job's friend, in offering encouragement, speaks prophetically into his life when he says: *Your beginnings will seem humble, so prosperous will your future be* (8.7) and, *He (God) will yet fill your mouth with laughter…* (8.21) while the godless will wither quicker than grass or a broken spider's web (8.12-15).

Then, in his quest for acceptance by God and for assurance

of eternal salvation, he asks the big question: *But how can a mortal be righteous before God?* (9.2.) Even the godly Job cannot claim acceptance with God on the basis of his own goodness – and there is plenty of that. Here he comes face to face with the heart of the gospel, which says that *all have sinned and come short of the glory of God, and are justified freely by his grace through the redemption that came by Christ Jesus* (Roman 3.23f).

Imagining a courtroom, Job pleads: *If only there were someone to arbitrate between us…someone to remove God's rod from me…* (9.33f). And there is indeed Someone who bears the wrath of God on our behalf as judgment for our sins.

As the Apostle John put it: *If anyone does sin, we have an advocate (one who speaks to the Father in our defence) – Jesus Christ, the Righteous One. He is the atoning sacrifice for our sins…* (1 John 2.1f). What an amazing promise, and Job was here looking ahead to the greatest event the world has known.

This is followed by a bout of introspection and self-pity for which you could hardly blame him under the circumstances. He was effectively saying, 'I wish I had never been born' (see 10.19).

But Zophar, another friend, held out hope for a time when many would court his favour (11.18f) and Job famously declares: *Though he slay me, yet will I hope in him,* anticipating the death and resurrection of Christ while also reflecting the refusal to compromise of Shadrach, Meshach and Abednego when faced with the fiery furnace by choosing worship of the true God over idolatry. Though condemned to a hellish death, they were sure God would rescue them. *But even if he does not,* they told the King, *we want you to know that we will not serve your gods or worship the image of gold you have set up* (Daniel 3.18).

In the same way, Job was sure that such firm commitment

to his Lord would turn out for his deliverance. Jesus said: *For whoever wants to save his life (or soul) will lose it, but whoever loses his life for me and for the gospel will save it* (Mark 8.35). God doesn't just want our prayers. He wants us to give up control of our lives, to forsake our independence and trust him completely – that is what he means by losing your life; you are losing it to him, and in doing so gaining everlasting life – *life that is truly life* (1 Timothy 6.19). In losing all (of yourself), you gain everything you need for a life full of meaning and purpose (see John 10.10).

This is followed by a series of Messianic allusions as Job contemplates his pitiful state as one who is scorned and jeered and struck on the cheek, turned over to evil men and even pierced, as Jesus was to experience on the cross (see 16.10-13). Speaking prophetically of Golgotha obviously without knowing it, he goes on: *... My days are cut short... surely mockers surround me...a man in whose face people spit* (17.1-6).

Bildad takes this even further, unwittingly describing Jesus' substitutionary sacrifice for our sins in musing over Job's fate as reaping the punishment reserved for the ungodly – certainly in the minds of the ancient world – that of leaving no offspring or descendants (18.19f). Like Jesus, Job suffered the lot of the wicked. *And who can speak of his descendants?* (Isa 53.8). Here, Isaiah prophesied of the Saviour who left no children (in the physical sense of course), *For he was cut off from the land of the living*. As many were appalled at Job's fate (18.20), many were appalled at the disfigured face of Jesus on the cross (Isa 52.14).

Job is tormented and tortured by the reproach of his friends and would rather have their pity for his state. *For the hand of God has struck me,* (19.21) he laments after describing himself in terms that conjure up pictures of the Holocaust: *I am nothing but skin and bones; I have escaped only by the skin of my teeth* (19.20).

Some Jews, perhaps looking to avoid the obvious conclusion, suggest that Isaiah 53 is a depiction of the Shoah. But while Jesus would surely have felt every inch of the pain of his people's mass murder, this is ultimately a picture of the Suffering Servant who would be the Saviour of both Jew and non-Jew alike.

And indeed God's hand was both in Job's torment and that of the Messiah, for he had something better in mind that could not be achieved any other way. As Isaiah said, *It was the Lord's will to crush him and cause him to suffer...* (Isa 53.10). Death is followed by resurrection, suffering by glory. *After the suffering of his soul, he will see the light of life and be satisfied...and will justify many and bear their iniquities* (Isa 53.11).

This leads to what, for me, is the climax of the book, the most sublime passage forever etched on the musical minds of those who love Handel's *Messiah* – the statement made by Job that, when all is said and done, he will see God: *I know that my Redeemer lives, and that he will stand at the latter day upon the earth* (19.25).

What a thrilling triumph as he takes a peek at perhaps the most momentous event of all time – the return of Jesus to Jerusalem as King of kings, when he places his feet on the Mount of Olives in fulfilment of the prophecy of Zechariah 14.4 (and implied in Acts 1.11f).

Job goes on: *And after my skin has been destroyed* (a possible reference to Israel's rising out of the ashes of the Holocaust), *yet in my flesh I will see God; I myself will see him with my own eyes...* (19.26f). This looks forward to the climax of the ages – the coming of the Messiah in power and great glory (see Matthew 24.30).

But a reality check follows, with the help of his friend Zophar – that the way of the wicked leads to destruction, and pleasing God brings its rewards in spite of suffering along the road. *The mirth of the wicked is brief; the joy of the godless lasts but a moment* (20.5). Everlasting life – in all its fullness – awaits the godly. This was also a key focus of Isaiah's message. Urged to 'cry out', the prophet asked: *What shall I cry?* And the answer was: *All men are like grass, and all their glory is like the flowers of the field. The grass withers and the flowers fall...but the word of our God lasts forever* (Isa 40.6-8).

Man is only here for a moment of eternity, and all his glory will quickly fade away. *In the midst of his plenty, distress will overtake him* (20.22), which was very much Job's experience, even in his righteousness. But how much worse for the ungodly, like the rich fool in Jesus' parable, who have not been 'rich towards God' (Luke 12.20f). As Zophar put it, *When he has filled his belly, God will vent his burning anger against him...* (20.23).

Eliphaz then poses a series of questions that basically amount to asking what benefit there is in serving God. But after pondering this somewhat perverse thought, Job concludes that *he knows the way that I take; when he has tested me, I shall come forth as gold* (23.10). What a wonderful revelation, that out of the fiery furnace comes godly faith and fortune more precious than gold. This is echoed by the Apostle Peter when he encourages the Christians suffering dreadful persecution that their trials had come *so that your faith – of greater worth than gold, which perishes even though refined by fire – may be proved genuine and may result in praise, glory and honour when Jesus Christ is revealed* (1 Peter 1.7).

Job adds: *I have treasured the words of his mouth more than my daily bread* (23.12), reflecting the fundamental Old Testament truth quoted by Jesus during his temptations in the Wilderness, that *man shall not live by bread alone, but by every word that proceeds from the mouth of God* (see Deuteronomy 8.3, Matthew 4.4).

Further reflecting on this thought, Job adds that *God drags away the mighty by his power; though they become established, they have no assurance of life* (24.22). No life assurance! Only in Messiah can we know such assurance, for all who believe in him will not perish, but have eternal life (John 3.16). Without trusting in the sacrificial blood of Jesus for our eternal security, we will be *cut off like ears of corn* at the final harvest of souls (24.24).

Job ponders over the wonders of creation and science with the extraordinary observation for his time that *he (God) suspends the earth over nothing* (26.7). And he re-asserts his determination not to dishonour God through his troubles, committing himself not to speak wickedness or utter deceit, adding: *I will not deny my integrity. I will maintain my righteousness and never let go of it; my conscience will not reproach me as long as I live* (27.4-6).

He meditates over the lengths to which man will go in search of earthly treasure, digging into the farthest recesses and darkness of the earth to extract nuggets of gold and other precious stones and metals. *But where can wisdom be found?* (28.12) *It cannot be bought with the gold of Ophir... the price of wisdom is beyond rubies* (28.16-18). And he concludes: *The fear of the Lord – that is wisdom...* (28.28), a truth repeated several times in the Scriptures.

Job continues his spiritual health check, recalling how he had rescued the poor, the fatherless and the widow, the blind and the lame as he sought to administer justice (29.12-17), prefiguring the call of Messiah to bring good news to the poor (see Isaiah 61.1-3) and healing to the sick. And yet, as with Jesus, he is mocked (30.1). He has not put his trust in gold; his security is with God (31.24). He does not rejoice at his enemy's misfortune (31.29) and has even made a covenant with his eyes *not to look lustfully at a girl* (31.1), pre-empting the revolutionary teaching of Jesus that so doing – and not just the act itself – was tantamount to committing adultery. (See Matthew 5.28.)

Nevertheless, all our righteousness is not enough to justify ourselves before a holy God. In fact, our best deeds are as 'filthy rags' to God (Isaiah 64.6). So Elihu, who has been waiting patiently to have his say, in deference to Job and his three friends who were his elders, was bursting to proclaim the answer to all the many questions – that God has provided a way for salvation; it is not something we can achieve by ourselves – it is the gift of God, so that no-one can boast (see also Ephesians 2.8f). And the sacrifice is provided by the blood of the Passover Lamb, who is the ultimate fulfilment of the sacrificial system carried out in the Jewish Temple.

Only through his sprinkled blood is there forgiveness of sins, but each of us must apply his blood to our own hearts, just as the Israelite slaves in Egypt daubed the doorposts and lintels of their houses with the blood of the lamb. Only thus were they forever freed from slavery to sin (see Hebrews 7.27, 10.10).

All this emphasis on God's provision for our righteousness (100% his, not even 1% of our own) is to keep us from pride (33.17), the worst of sins. In the words of the old hymn *Rock of Ages*, 'Nothing in my hand I bring, simply to the cross I cling'. Through God's great provision – his only Son, our Messiah – we are ransomed, restored and redeemed from the pit of death to the light of life (33.24-30).

Elihu views Job as voicing what was to be Jeremiah's complaint: *Why does the way of the wicked prosper?* (Jer 12.1). Or, more specifically, making the point that *it profits a man nothing when he tries to please God* (34.9). Or so it seems. But Elihu speaks of hope ahead and of the greatness of God, which is beyond our understanding (36.16 & 26).

The Almighty does indeed speak (33.14), through the glory of his creation for example (37.5), and then answers Job directly out of the storm (38.1) with questions of his own: *Who is this that darkens my counsel with words without knowledge?* (38.2), and then: ... *Have you comprehended the vast expanses of the earth?* (38.18). The world does not revolve around us. *Does the eagle soar at your command?* (39.27) ...*Would you condemn me to justify yourself?* (40.8) Do we argue with God to vindicate our wrongdoing? This may not apply to Job, but it does to most of us.

There follows a magnificent description of a crocodile (41), known then as a leviathan, presumably for the purpose of making the point that you cannot tame God, as I have already mentioned. He is not your pet, as some gruesome newspaper stories of man-eating reptiles have recently illustrated. *If you lay a hand on him, you will remember the struggle and never do it again!* (41.8) ... *Who dares open the doors of his mouth, ringed about with his fearsome teeth?* (41.14) ...*Nothing on earth is his equal – a creature without fear. He looks down on all that are haughty; he is king over all that are proud* (41.33f).

Job got the drift of God's message, replying: *I know that you can do all things; no plan of yours can be thwarted* (42.2). He realises that he spoke out of turn of things he did not understand, and repents in dust and ashes, having confessed: *My ears had heard of you but now my eyes have seen you* (42.5) – the testimony of all those who have had a true encounter with the risen Lord.

And after Job prayed for his friends, whom the Lord scolded for not speaking of him as Job had done, he received a double portion of prosperity – a dirty word in some Christian circles, but in truth it *is* one of the ways God blesses us. However, the corollary is also true – that lack of blessing, as Job also experienced in great measure, is neither a sign that God has forsaken us nor that we are living unrighteous lives before him.

David Pawson makes the interesting point that if sin and suffering were directly related, we would be forced to be godly for purely selfish reasons; love for God and people would not be voluntary – see *Unlocking the Bible* (Collins, 2003, re-launched in 2007), p433.

Job was duly blessed with great riches – 14,000 sheep, 6,000 camels and a lot more – as well as with many more children (as many as he had before, in fact); seven sons and three daughters. And the daughters were the most beautiful in the land. They get a special mention, and were even granted an inheritance along with their brothers – unusual for the time.

The Lord blessed the latter part of Job's life more than the first (42.12). What a wonderful conclusion to this outstanding test of fiery trials. It resonates with me too, though I do not claim to have suffered anything remotely comparable to Job. But I *can* truly testify that if, through thick and thin, you refuse to deny the Lord and fully commit to serving him with integrity and conscience intact no matter what, you will inevitably finish up more blessed than you were at the beginning.

CHAPTER 6 – TWO BEAUTIFUL WOMEN

*The story of Ruth and Esther, who both came to the aid of
the Jewish people: one a Gentile, the other a Jew.*

Both these women present a big challenge to us, and their
biographies remind us that we can all make a huge difference
to the world around us – whether for good or evil.

Esther, or Hadassah, is presented as the beautiful young
woman who, as Queen, saved the Jews from annihilation in
ancient Persia – which just happens to be the equivalent of
modern-day Iran, posing a similar threat today. Unlike Ruth,
Esther was Jewish, though her nationality was withheld at
the time of her accession to the throne as the potential for
anti-Semitism was so great that the Bible's account of her
heroics only mentions God in code – skilfully woven into
the text through acrostics, according to respected theologian
David Pawson.[1]

Esther was evidently an orphan brought up by her elder
cousin Mordecai neither of whose names are Hebrew. Her
call to royalty came as a result of the disrespect shown
by her predecessor Queen Vashti to her husband. It was
considered important that she should be a good role model
for all the women in the land, so that they would respect
their husbands (1.20) and every man be ruler over his own
household. A noble ethos that our present rulers could well
try adopting. For example, the sheer thuggery demonstrated
by hard-left politicians at the helm of Her Majesty's Official
Opposition (and I am talking of Britain's Queen, not ancient
Persia's) is undoubtedly linked to an unprecedented rise in
knife crime on our streets – these leaders are hardly ideal
role models for our youth!

So King Xerxes made a search of "beautiful young virgins" to replace her and Esther won the pageant, though I suspect her inner beauty also played a part (2.17 – see also 1 Peter 3.4).

Then Mordecai uncovered a plot to assassinate the king and reported the guilty officers, who were duly hanged. But the king was not at this stage aware of the Jew's role in saving his skin. So when Haman rose to prominence and sought the king's consent to destroy the Jews in his empire – vexed by Mordecai's refusal to ingratiate himself before him by kneeling down in his presence as he demanded – he took out his vengeance on all God's people (3.6) and cast the lot (pur) for a date when the pogrom should take place. I imagine that Mordecai saw kneeling down in this way as a form of worship, and therefore idolatrous.

Please note Haman's reasoning for destroying the Jews – that it wasn't in the king's best interest to tolerate people whose customs were different to those of everyone else and who did not obey the king's laws (3.8). Sound familiar? We (Christians and Jews) are now beginning to face a similar reality in our day as political correctness takes hold.

So when news of this plot emerged, Mordecai persuaded Esther to intervene, but she knew that anyone who approached the king in the inner court without being summoned would be put to death – unless he held out a golden sceptre. It would be very dangerous.

Mordecai challenged Esther: *Do not think that because you are in the king's house you alone of all the Jews will escape. For if you remain silent at this time, relief and deliverance for the Jews will arise from another place,[2] but you and your father's family will perish. And who knows but that you have come to royal position for such a time as this?*

Esther had to be challenged by the threat to her people's existence. In a similar way in more modern times, the journalist Theodor Herzl was challenged by the anti-Semitism he witnessed in Paris, where he was correspondent for an Austrian newspaper, to launch the Zionist movement pushing for the re-settling of their ancient land, where they could be safe.

Esther ordered a three-day fast and promised: *When this is done, I will go to the king, even though it is against the law. And if I perish, I perish* (4.16). One is reminded of the fiery furnace experienced by Shadrach, Meshach and Abednego who effectively said the same thing, and survived the ordeal (see Daniel 3.16-18).

Just as Esther risked her life for her people, so should we be prepared to die for our Lord and his people. In modern Persia, meanwhile, the ayatollahs are determined to wipe Israel off the map, using nuclear weapons if necessary, while continuing to sponsor terror groups Hezbollah and Hamas (note the similarity of the name with Haman) on the Jewish state's borders.

I was recently reminded of the power of a three-day fast. When an Arab family from Nazareth took this on shortly after they had come to believe in Yeshua in 2007, a relative was miraculously healed of cancer!

After the fast, Esther held a banquet for Haman – on successive days – but this generous gesture failed to assuage his fury at Mordecai's continued snub. So he built a gallows on which to hang him.

Then the king learnt that it was Mordecai who had exposed the plot to assassinate him (6.2) and realised he had not been suitably honoured. Just as Haman was about to inform the king of the gallows he had built for Mordecai, he was instead humiliated by being forced to carry out a ceremony in honour of the Jew, dressing him in a royal robe and placing him on one of the king's horses. Esther subsequently pleaded for her people to be spared and the tables were turned (9.1) on the perpetrator of the plot to kill the Jews, especially when he was discovered molesting the king's wife. Zeresh, Haman's wife, who had suggested he build the gallows, now says: *Since Mordecai, before whom your downfall has started, is of Jewish origin, you cannot stand against him – you will surely come to ruin!* (6.13).

Those who dare to stand against the Jews or their Messiah will surely – sooner or later – come to ruin! If God is for you, who can be against you? (See Romans 8.31.) Haman would now be hanged on the gallows he had erected for Mordecai. He had literally made a rope with which to hang himself, as the saying goes. And the evil scheme he had devised against the Jews had now "come back on to his own head" (9.25). God wreaked vengeance on all their enemies in the land while the Jews engaged in joy and feasting, and to this day annual Purim celebrations are held when gifts are exchanged, as we do at Christmas.

As a result of this mighty vindication of God's chosen, "many people of other nationalities became Jews because fear of the Jews had seized them" (8.17).

It's important also to note that Haman was an Agagite, a descendant of the Amalekites who, for no reason, had attacked the Israelites when they came out of Egypt, and were still a thorn in their side because King Saul had disobeyed the Lord's command to wipe them out (see 1 Samuel 15). Now they came back to haunt them and they are still causing trouble today. The lesson from this: do everything the Lord commands. Whatever he says, do it!

In the modern era, the tables were turned on Germany, who made the grave mistake of touching the apple of God's eye (Zech 2.8). And it all came back on their own heads as their cities were reduced to rubble – Darmstadt, for instance, had its own 9/11 when, on September 11th 1944, the city was destroyed, leaving 12,000 dead and many more homeless.

The sick anti-Semitism within Britain's Labour Party will ultimately come down on its own head with similar destructive force and was, in my opinion, the key reason for their virtual wipe-out in the December 2019 election.

Mordecai became second in rank to the king, as Joseph had been similarly elevated to high position in Egypt, although in his case he had been betrayed by his own brothers. But even then, as now with Mordecai, what was meant for evil, God intended for good (see Genesis 50.20).

Esther's plea to the king on behalf of her people is also a wonderful picture of our own deliverance from sin and death by the sacrifice of Jesus, through which we are accepted into the presence of the King of kings. In holding out his golden sceptre, the king signified acceptance of Esther's presence which she then acknowledged by touching the tip of the sceptre. Jesus, on the throne of heaven, holds out his 'sceptre of righteousness' (Hebrews 1.8) which, if we allow to touch our hearts, will grant us access into the most holy place.

But we must make our presence felt, acknowledging our need. We must knock on the door and make our request. Have you asked Jesus into your life? *Let us then approach God's throne of grace with confidence, so that we may receive mercy and find grace to help us in our time of need* (Hebrews 4.16).

A little afterthought… Perhaps I am reading too much into the text, but I could not help noticing the "blue and white" descriptions of linen hanging in the royal garden (1.6) as well as being the colours of royal garments (8.15). The flag of modern Israel is of a Star of David on a blue and white background! God was surely planning Jewish restoration even before their mass exodus to the four corners of the earth.

****

Now let us take a look at the story of Ruth. As an incurable romantic, I love this little book which has made an impact on the world out of all proportion to its brevity. It is the remarkable record of how a young Gentile widow became the ancestor of the Jewish Messiah, our Lord Jesus Christ, and teaches us that we too can make a profound impact on our world with a faith like hers that is totally committed to serving the God of Israel.

The background to her story was the exile of Naomi and Ruth's late father-in-law Elimelech, along with their two sons, due to a famine. The irony was that they lived in Bethlehem (meaning *House of Bread*) in Judah, where they should have had plenty to eat. But famine in the Bible is generally a sign of divine punishment, and there is no indication in the text that the family had prayed or sought God over why they were being so judged. We know that repentance would have brought about a positive result. Anyway, they relocated to Moab, on the far side of the Dead Sea and among ancient Israel's adversaries, to seek for greener grass, as it were. Things did not go too well. Naomi's husband died and, to add to her deep distress, so did her two sons who had married Moabite women Ruth and Orpah.

Naomi is the feminine of Noach which means 'comfort' but, after suffering such grievous loss, she asked to be called Mara instead, which means 'bitter'. In any case, she had had enough and duly packed her bags and set out for home back in Bethlehem. Sounds a bit familiar, doesn't it? They had set out for a far country, where things went from bad to worse, until they came to their senses and decided to return to the Father's house, where food was plentiful.

Naomi tried to persuade her two daughters-in-law to stay in the region and get re-married, possibly because she judged they would have had less chance in Judah, where the men would have been disinclined to marry outside their clan. But

Ruth clings to her mother-in-law, determined to honour her and her people, and follow her to the Promised Land. She had evidently acquired Naomi's faith and chosen to shelter under the wings of the God of Israel, humbly choosing the better way, declaring: *Wherever you go, I go... your people shall be my people, and your God, my God* (Ruth 1.16). Like Abraham, she did not know where she was going but recognised in Naomi the true path to God, and would be 'richly rewarded' (2.12) beyond her wildest dreams for her great faith.

The Bible says: *No eye has seen, no ear has heard, no mind has conceived what God has prepared for those who love him* (1 Corinthians 2.9, Isaiah 64.4).

How amazing: even though a Gentile, she would become an essential part of the genealogy of the Jewish Messiah, the Son of God! Her love, her loyalty and her kindness for her Jewish mother-in-law was richly rewarded indeed – apparently loyalty and love are almost the same word in Hebrew.

Here is another thought: she had left her father and mother and homeland to pursue God's calling. And what does Jesus say about this? Matthew 19.29... *Everyone who has left houses or brothers or sisters or father or mother or children or fields for my sake will receive a hundred times as much and will inherit eternal life.*

By inviting Christ into our lives, we too shelter under the shadow of the wings of the God of Israel, the One who, in Jesus, is the way, the truth and the life. We go where they go! Even today, if you stand up for the Jews and honour them, you invite ridicule, perhaps even death threats – certainly demonic attack – for doing so. Just ask former Labour Friends of Israel chair Joan Ryan MP, who received death threats and the most appalling abuse after resigning from the party over anti-Semitism, along with several others.

Dutchwoman Corrie ten Boom was sent to a concentration camp for protecting the Jews from the Nazis and had to watch her sister being murdered there.

It is costly, for sure, but the church needs to recover her love for the Jews, or we are going nowhere – there will be no revival. If we fail to bless the seed of Abraham, we will certainly not be 'richly rewarded' by revival. We will actually come under a curse.

Ruth was moved to lay at the feet of Boaz as he rested after the threshing of the barley harvest. This was regarded at the time as a sort of unspoken proposal – by warming a man's feet, you were making the fairly bold suggestion that you would not mind being married to him!

It also brings to mind two examples of great devotion for Jesus recorded in the New Testament – the prostitute who wet our Lord's feet with her tears, not to mention expensive perfume (Luke 7.38 & 44), and Mary who sat at the Lord's feet refusing to be distracted by the household chores (Luke 10.38-42).

Boaz, for his part, already impressed by Ruth's kindness, is now also flattered by her attention as there were plenty of younger men available, in his view. Clearly, she was still a beautiful young woman. But he does the right thing by first offering her hand to his older brother, who qualified as a closer kinsman but could see that Boaz was smitten and gave his consent in the customary way by taking off his sandal and giving it to his younger sibling.

Following Jesus is not a cakewalk. We have to give up ownership of our life and hand it over to Jesus, taking up his cross – and in losing it, we save it (see Mark 8.35). Ruth left behind her life in Moab, but she gained so much more, even becoming the great-grandmother of King David and the ancestor of our Messiah (see Matthew 10.37-39).

Indeed, she also gained a husband of high standing,

Boaz, through whom she gave birth to Obed. Boaz was her kinsman-redeemer, a relative who, through marriage, enabled her to re-inherit property to which her offspring would be entitled in the year of jubilee (every 50 years), when land ownership had to be returned to the original family. As kinsman-redeemer, Boaz also illustrated the way Jesus became our redeemer by purchasing our redemption through his body on the cross, where his blood paid the price for our sins.

Back to the comparison with the Prodigal Son parable, notice that when they first returned to Bethlehem – the Father's 'house of bread' from which they had been driven away by famine – there was plenty to eat and, in fact, all they needed for life. The Father had even prepared a feast – the barley harvest was beginning just as they arrived (see 1.22).

Notice too how Ruth was prepared to pick up the leftover grain. And yet, because of her commitment to Naomi along with her kindness and loyalty, they had all they needed to eat – and more. We also recall how the Canaanite woman was prepared to eat the crumbs that fell from the Master's table, and how she was commended for her great faith despite Jesus' emphasis that he had come for the lost sheep of Israel (see Matthew 15.21-28). But he honoured the faith of this Gentile woman, who was greatly rewarded with the healing of her suffering daughter.

Yes, the Lord sees us while we are still far off, and comes running out to meet us (Luke 15), and even throws a party for us. He promises that if anyone is hungry (John 6.35) or thirsty (John 7.37), he will meet their need, as he did with Ruth, who also had plenty to drink (2.9). Boaz would even give her 'anything she asked' (3.11), a promised Jesus also made (John 16.23) to those wholly committed to him.

And in answer to the prayers of the elders, her offspring helped to build up the house of Israel and indeed 'became famous in Bethlehem' (4.11), and all this through a daughter-in-law who was better to Naomi than seven sons (see 4.15).

It is an amazing story, how God chose this gentle, kind and humble Moabitess to be part of his royal line. And yet it is hardly the sort of lineage we would choose. God's ways are not our ways (Isaiah 55.8); in his economy, the first shall be last, and the last first. The proud are humbled, and the humble are exalted. Boaz was actually the son of Rahab, the prostitute, who hid the spies in Jericho's wall and was possibly the first Gentile in the land of Canaan to embrace the God of Israel. Boaz was also the descendant of Judah, one of the twelve sons of Jacob, and is also descended from Tamar who had offspring after she was raped.

No wonder Jesus became known as the 'friend of sinners'. Yet he loves us too much to leave us as we are, raising us up to be so much more than our human frailty would have allowed. You too can change your world by following Jesus, the Jew, and honouring and blessing his people.

Anyway, here are two wonderful women who, in God's perfect timing, came to royal position – to save, and to bless, his people. As we honour them, may we also be inspired to follow their example of faith and fortitude, forsaking all as they risked their lives in His Majesty's Service.

[1] *Unlocking the Bible*, p.677

[2] *Another place* is an idiom for God or heaven, according to theologian Dr Fred Wright. If so, it challenges the general perception that God is not mentioned in the book.

CHAPTER 7 – BIBI AND THE BIBLE

I mentioned Benjamin 'Bibi' Netanyahu earlier as a Bible-believer, and this is key for an Israeli leader for, as he once made clear in a powerful speech to the UN, Israel's right to exist and prosper as a nation is rooted in God's Word – the same word that tells us all about Jesus, as we have been discovering. The destiny of Gentile Christians and the land and people of Israel is emphatically bound together. But this also brings responsibility for both groups to work out their destiny in the light of the God of Israel, whom we worship, and his laws.

So, with Bibi and the Bible in mind, I want to make the point that Israel is responsible for the Law (the moral law, that is) as well as the Land. As the earth is ravaged by an unprecedented series of natural disasters, accompanied with threats of war and terror, world leaders were recently presented with a heavenly vision.

In challenging the 'fake history' of those who deny Jewish links with Israel's holiest sites, Mr Netanyahu sounded a clarion call for the United Nations to acknowledge the divine authority of the world's greatest book – the Bible.[1]

Three times he referenced the Bible in his speech at the UN. Referring to a declaration in July of that year of Hebron's Tomb of the Patriarchs as a Palestinian World Heritage site, he said you won't read the true facts of its history in the latest UNESCO (United Nations Educational, Scientific and Cultural Organization) report. "But you can read about it in a somewhat weightier publication – it's called the Bible," he mocked, adding that it was "a great read", that he read it every week, and that they could purchase it from Amazon.[2]

How refreshing that at least one nation's leader takes his stand on the Bible, though it is entirely appropriate in this case as Bibi (at the time of writing) still leads the people who gave it to us! As well as being a sacred book written by divine authority, it is also an historical record which validates Israel's claim to the Promised Land they now once again inhabit. But in making such a divine claim for the territory, Bibi must also seek to apply the Law – that is, the Lord's teaching on ethical matters – to his domain.

He is right in saying that the words of the prophet Isaiah – that God called Israel to be a light to the nations – is being fulfilled as the tiny Jewish state becomes a rising power. But their call "to bring salvation to the ends of the earth" (see Isaiah 49.6) must mean more than hi-tech innovation and being good neighbours through their search-and-rescue teams sent to disaster areas and medics tending to wounded Syrians on their northern border, though we praise God for all that.

Notwithstanding all this, Israel is rife with immorality – and I am thinking particularly about abortion, a killing of innocents that echoes previous turning points in Israel's (and the world's) history at the time of Moses and of Jesus. I appreciate that its practice in modern Israel is less prevalent than in most parts of the West,[3] but some 650,000 children[4] have nevertheless been denied life in a country that gave God's law to the world, including the commandment 'Thou shall not kill'.

Paradoxically, the killing of innocents has accompanied the greatest rescues mankind has witnessed. Moses survived the edict of the Egyptian Pharaoh calling for the slaughter of all Hebrew babies to lead his people out of slavery to the Promised Land. Yeshua, the Jewish Messiah, survived King Herod's massacre of infants – ironically by fleeing with his family to Egypt in response to God's warning – to bring salvation to the world through his sacrificial death on a Roman cross outside Jerusalem.

Moses also received the Law of God; now Jesus writes the Law on our hearts (see Ezekiel 36.26, Jeremiah 31.33). Moses was hidden among the bulrushes of the Nile and became the saviour of his people; Jesus was raised in the backwaters of Nazareth but became the Saviour of the world as he brought true freedom to all who would trust in his redeeming blood (see John 8.36).

My colleague Dr Clifford Denton tells me of a conference held in Israel in 1996 at which Messianic leaders gathered to discuss the Jewish roots of Christianity. "Unknown to me until afterwards," he said, "it turned out that the Knesset (Israel's parliament) was voting on an abortion law at the very same time that we were discussing Torah (the Law of Moses). In fact, the Knesset was struck by lightning at that very time."

With innocents around the world being butchered as never before, the Messiah is about to be revealed to the nations. Jesus indicated that his coming again would be as in the days of Noah (see Luke 17.26) when the world was full of violence (see Genesis 6.13). Terrorism stalks the planet as unbelievable cruelty mars even supposedly enlightened societies, while nuclear holocausts have become a distinct possibility, with both North Korea and Iran making ominous noises. All this while nations reel under the ferocious effects of earthquakes and hurricanes – also spoken of as signs of the Messiah's imminent return (see Luke 21.25-28), especially when they follow in rapid succession and increasing severity, as on a woman with labour pains (see Matthew 24.8).

Of the three major Jewish feasts, Jesus has fulfilled both Passover and Pentecost. Many Bible commentators believe he will soon also fulfil the Feast of Tabernacles when he returns to reign from Jerusalem. The One who protects his people, and provides for them, as he did in the Wilderness so long ago, will finally bring in the harvest of those who believe in him as he comes to 'tabernacle' (or live/make his dwelling) among us (see John 1.14).

The day is coming when the killing of innocents will give way to the glorious return of the Son of Man "coming in a cloud with power and great glory" (Luke 21.27) to avenge every wrong as he passes judgment on a cruel world. Israel – you are truly called to be a light to the nations, and indeed you have impressed so far with many marvellous inventions. But the brightest light is the fulfilment of the Law through YeshuaHaMashiach, who brings hope, not despair; and life, not death.

Sword, or the Lord?
We continue to explore the theme of Israel's calling to the nations. With all the threats she is now facing, it is perfectly understandable that Israel should be sharpening their swords as they prepare for the worst the enemy can throw at them. A strong defence force is certainly necessary. But an even more serious danger is that they should rely on the power of their weapons, or indeed on their own strength of will and character, along with their growing expertise in military innovations. It is dangerous because it demonstrates that they are relying on what the Bible refers to as "horses and chariots" rather than on the Lord who called them, as his chosen people, to be a light to the Gentiles.

For it is only when we trust the Lord with all our hearts and not our own understanding that God will give us the guidance we need in order to tread the path for which he has destined us (see Proverbs 3.5f). As one who loves Israel, I am at the same time not blind to the fact that many of its citizens lead a sinful lifestyle. This is no reason to withdraw support for the beleaguered nation, but they do need to repent of their waywardness and godlessness. As they have done so many times in their long history, they have absorbed the ways of the world around them – and so we witness political correctness here as elsewhere, most starkly seen in a defiance of sexual morality.

But they are the people of the Book, who gave the world the Bible, the Ten Commandments and Jesus himself. Now God is saying: do not wait until you are overrun by enemies before you turn back to the Lord who called you out of slavery in Egypt with a mighty hand. He urges you to trust him now!

I cannot recall why, but my wife and I were discussing Israel's sin, and whether God's judgment was inevitable, before turning to our daily reading which is our habit every morning. We use the *Every Day with Jesus* notes of the late Selwyn Hughes which focuses on a theme over a two-month period drawn together by a variety of different Scripture passages. So we opened the little book and found the text for the day was Hosea 14.1-3: *Return, Israel, to the Lord your God. Your sins have been your downfall* (v1). It goes on: *Assyria cannot save us; we will not mount warhorses...* (v3). [For Assyria, perhaps we should read America.]

The Lord was clearly in on our discussion and had a ready answer! Bear in mind that the prophet was concluding his book which pictures Israel as an adulterous wife who repeatedly runs after other men, breaking the first commandment that we should have no other gods in our lives. Self-reliance is thus the worst of sins because we put ourselves in God's place and we are saying we can live without him; that he is redundant. This is gross idolatry, and we must repent of it.

Notice, however, that in spite of their serial adultery, God has not forsaken Israel; he has not divorced the one he loves. He loves her with an everlasting love (Jer 31.3).

He has entered into a covenant relationship which cannot be broken. But we should not abuse his great faithfulness.

The recent archaeological find near Tel Aviv, suggesting human activity in the area half-a-million years ago, did not exactly excite me. Far more edifying was the August 2015 find in Gath, a city once occupied by Philistines who plotted against the Israelites, their sworn enemies, and the home of the infamous Goliath!

The huge gates uncovered by archaeologists were thought to be indestructible. But in an extraordinary battle in the Valley of Elah, a young man who trusted in the Lord brought down their giant leader with a single stone. Goliath defied the armies of Israel, but David responded: *Who is this uncircumcised Philistine that he should defy the armies of the living God?* (1 Samuel 17.26). And he taunted the giant: *You come against me with sword and spear and javelin, but I come against you in the name of the Lord Almighty, the God of the armies of Israel, whom you have defied* (1 Sam 17.45).

Like other nations, Israel needs to seek forgiveness from God for succumbing to the ways of the world as well as for their outright disobedience to his commandments. We need to move from independence – the great sin of the age – to reliance upon God. Isn't it time we heard Israel's leaders say, with great clarity and in defiance of political correctness, that we do not trust in sword or spear or javelin, nor even on our allies, but in the name of the Lord Almighty?

Having said all that, a weak Western church has not helped Jews to see Jesus for who he really is, and thus return to the God of Israel. According to a respected author, much of Western society has been bewitched by a political elite seeking to change the order of God's creation, with the result that the church has lamely retreated from the public square with a message that could otherwise challenge it. In *Gospel Culture* (Wilberforce Publications), Joseph Boot castigates many of today's Christians as being part of a "weak, ineffectual, intellectually impotent, compromised and complacent church culture of inward Christian pansies" by the way in which they have allowed the world to dictate how the church should be run.

And he concludes that much of the Western church has failed in its mission to bring the Word of God to every aspect of life. For the most part, he argues, we have subscribed to a heretical 'Two Kingdom' theology separating the sacred from the secular as a convenient excuse for not engaging with an apostate Western culture. We retreat into our holy huddles and dare not raise the issue of politics in our pulpits, with the result that congregations are rarely, if ever, encouraged to weigh topical debates in the light of Scripture.

But this is God's world, and the Bible speaks of all life – there is no big issue of our day on which it does not have something pertinent to say. Yet we have allowed the secularism and humanism of the political and media elite to influence how we think, so that we are now effectively conforming to the world rather than being "transformed by the renewal of our minds" as St Paul urged the church at Rome (see Romans 12.2).

Boot argues that today's political agenda is a resurgence of ancient witchcraft with its manipulative and brainwashing techniques. And many of our churches have been influenced by it. Disengaging from the public square was a "fatal flaw" which led to endless divisions among Christians "frantically drafting peace treaties with non-Christian thought".

I guess this is why I have struggled for 40 years to convince Christian leaders in Britain of the need for a media bringing a biblical worldview to mainstream debate. And I concur with the author's statement that "for us to deny that we have a task on the earth to apply his salvation victory and lordship, his beauty and truth to all aspects of life and thought is to renounce Christ."

Just because culture is being relentlessly driven in the opposite direction to gospel teaching does not mean we should not challenge it. It leaves the public at large not only alienated from God (and we are called through the gospel to reconcile man with God) but now seeking to alienate God's world from its Maker – "to separate what God joins and join what God separates". We desperately need a recovery of a truly scriptural view of life – "a full-orbed gospel" that takes God at his Word and understands and applies the implications of Christ's resurrection to all of life.

Boot writes: "If we are to understand the radical changes in our society today as inspired by diabolic principalities and manifest in ideological strongholds that set themselves up against the knowledge of God (Ephesians 6.12; 2 Corinthians 10.4-6), then we must grasp the essential instrumentality of modern political life as engaged, wittingly or not, in *witchcraft* – employing a 'secret' (elitist) knowledge in an attempt to join opposites." He further explains: "Our current culture is thus bent on defacing the image of God by denying that man is man and woman is woman, by negating the God-given nature of marriage and by politically manipulating people to believe and act as though an illusion were true – that homosexuality is normative, gender is fluid and that androgyny is the human ideal."

[1]*Christians United for Israel*, September 21 2017.
[2]Ibid.
[3]Among European nations, only Croatia has a lower abortion rate than Israel, according to the *Jerusalem Post* on March 31 2015. And on January 14th 2014 the *Times of Israel* reported that, despite liberal policies on the issue, the nation's abortion rate had been declining for the previous quarter-century, dropping 21% since 1990 to 20,063 in 2012 (or 117 for every 1,000 live births).
[4]*Johnston's Archive* compiled by Wm Robert Johnston, last updated February 25 2017.

CHAPTER 8 – AN UPSIDE-DOWN MEDIA

The problem with discussing the Bible, Christianity, and Israel is that they all suffer from a bad press, and so it is important to explore why this might be and how it all fits into the big picture. Asked to answer the question: *Is there really media bias against Israel in the West?* for the *Prophecy Today* online magazine (www.prophecytoday.uk), I responded with the following thoughts.

It has been rightly said that the pen is mightier than the sword; and just as this truth has been used to great effect for the good of the world, as in the case of gospel proclamation, so it also has the potential for spreading cancerous ideology like Marxism and atheism.

Lies repeated often enough become accepted as fact, as in Germany when its people were assailed by horrible misrepresentation of the Jews through Hitler's propaganda chief Joseph Goebbels. And the same applies to the distorted narrative on Israel's legitimacy since Arab-Muslim fanatics took over the baton from the Nazis.

As a result, much of the mainstream media in the West has swallowed an upside-down version of Middle East political realities, ignoring historical facts while choosing instead to believe the mantra that Israel has no right to exist, that they have stolen Arab land and have no historic link to the region.

Attitudes to Israel become both illogical and irrational, so that legitimate defence under the provocation of constant rocket fire is deemed disproportionate if, for example, more are killed on the aggressor's side than on the nation defending itself – as if it should be some sort of handicap competition.

And I believe that rising anti-Semitism in Britain is built around this oft-repeated media narrative, invented by 'Palestinian nationalism', depicting tiny Israel as the Middle East bully. In a nutshell, its ultimate goal is the destruction of Israel. Having failed to achieve this in the three major conventional wars between the Jewish state and its Arab neighbours (1948, 1967 & 1973), Palestinian leaders adopted a new and increasingly effective strategy – to demonise Israel internationally, particularly in the eyes of Western liberal opinion, by re-branding the conflict as a heroic struggle for Palestinian freedom and self-determination against an oppressive 'occupying' power.[1]

In reality, the real purpose behind the creation of a Palestinian state in the West Bank and Gaza is to provide a launch pad for an eventual 'second phase' war of extermination against an Israel psychologically weakened by decades of terrorism, economic sanctions and diplomatic isolation. Violence against Jews is constantly encouraged through Palestinian and Arab media. If you wish to check this out, visit the website of the Middle East Media Research Institute at http://www.memri.org which monitors Arab and wider Islamic media and posts video clips with English translations of material originally appearing in Arabic, Farsi, Turkish or some other Middle Eastern tongue.

In addition, the Palestinian Media Watch – http://www. palwatch.org – focuses specifically on Palestinian media output, which recycles classic anti-Jewish conspiracy theories and employs the same kind of abusive language and stereotypes used by the Nazis to justify the Holocaust.

What is more, the official PA logo brazenly shows a map of a future Palestinian state stretching from the Jordan River to the Mediterranean, clearly indicating that there is no likelihood of their being satisfied with a 'two-state solution' in the long term.

Mainstream media coverage of the conflict is typically biased against Israel in its failure to tell the historical truth about that conflict, its uncritical acceptance of the narrative of Palestinian 'victimhood', its failure to report and analyse the failures of Palestinian leaders and institutions, and its failure to reveal the degree to which truthful reporting of Hamas activity in Gaza, for example, has been hampered or prevented by the intimidation of journalists.

This general media bias also reveals itself in the disproportionate coverage of Israel's shortcomings, real or imagined, compared with the relative lack of scrutiny of the mass carnage and tyranny which prevails in much of the Arab-Islamic world.

For example, Italian reporter Gabriel Barbati disclosed that Israel was telling the truth and Hamas was lying when he confirmed that the deaths of ten people at the Al-Shati refugee camps on July 28th 2014 was not the result of Israeli fire, as had been widely reported (and in the case of *NBC* never corrected), but of a misfired Hamas missile.

But he only disclosed this information once he was out of Gaza, beyond the reach of Hamas retaliation. Not surprisingly, truth has been the first casualty of Hamas intimidation and manipulation of the international press. All of this anti-Israel bias is further complicated by the toxic mix of political affiliations we are witnessing these days, exacerbated by the misleading comments of politicians who are understandably quoted in view of their status.

At the same time a worldwide revival of radical Islam is wreaking havoc across much of Central Asia, Europe and Africa. And the likes of ISIS share a hatred of Israel with the Palestinian parties Fatah and Hamas, which leaves the West's pro-Palestinian lobby in cahoots with the very people who are trying to destroy our way or life.

Yet despite clear evidence to the contrary, former British

Prime Minister David Cameron tried to convince us that Islam is a peaceful religion, whereas he was actually bowing to political correctness and fear. This is a repeat of what happened during the British Mandate of Palestine, when murderous threats saw the British government capitulate to Arab demands at the cost of Jewish lives and aspirations.

So it is that today our politicians and media dare not rock the boat by facing up to reality. That radical Islam represents a threat to our society seems patently obvious, especially since 9/11 and 7/7. But we continue to sweep this bad news under the carpet. Even evangelical Christian publications shy off tackling the issue, as I have discovered through my own experience. One magazine was keen for me to help them in my retirement, but backed away after my very first submission – a topical article on the threat of Islam.

Those who wish to silence such truths find themselves in league with the Hard Left, who in turn have joined forces with the Far Right Islamist cause opposing both the people of Israel and the God of Israel – hence the reason Christians also become a target.

But thinking people in the Muslim world are challenging the status quo – for example, a newscaster in Saudi Arabia called on fellow Muslims to stop pretending that there is no connection between the teachings of Islam and the violent attacks we are increasingly having to witness.

The various camps betray such bizarre contradictions. Someone tweeted that, though liberal media like *The Guardian* are quick to rally to the Palestinian cause, it doesn't seem to occur to them that they are taking sides with what a survey has discovered to be an extremely homophobic society.[2]

But as the prophet Isaiah wrote some 2,700 years ago: *Woe to those who call evil good and good evil, who put darkness for light and light for darkness, who put bitter for sweet and sweet for bitter* (Isaiah 5.20). Perhaps Shakespeare had this in mind when he wrote the witches' incantation in Macbeth: "Fair is foul and foul is fair, hover through the fog and filthy air..."

Talking of *The Guardian* in a more positive light, it was one of their highly-respected veteran journalists who exposed the absurd media portrayal of Israel as an 'apartheid' state for the nonsense that it is. Having worked as a correspondent in South Africa for 26 years, and having lived in Israel for 17, Benjamin Pogrund made it clear that there could be no comparison; that Israel is not remotely like that.

"Dragging in the emotive word 'apartheid' is not only incorrect but creates confusion and distracts from the main issue," he wrote.[3] And referring to the security barrier – originally built to keep out suicide bombers – as the 'apartheid wall' was "untrue propaganda".

"Of course Israel isn't perfect, despite its many and wondrous achievements since 1948. However, for critics it's not enough to denounce its ills and errors: instead, they exaggerate and distort and present an ugly caricature far distant from reality."

So why, he asks, is the apartheid accusation pushed so relentlessly, especially by the Boycott, Divestment and Sanctions (BDS) movement?

"I believe campaigners want Israel declared an apartheid state so it becomes a pariah, open to the world's severest sanctions. Many want not just an end to the occupation but an end to Israel itself.

"Tragically, some well-intentioned, well-meaning people in Britain and other countries are falling for the BDS line without realising what they are actually supporting. BDS campaigners and other critics need to be questioned: Why do they single out Israel, above all others, for a torrent of false propaganda? Why is Israel the only country in the world whose very right to existence is challenged in this way?"

[1] See *In Defence of Israel*, Philip Vander Elst, May 2015
[2] *Peace in Jerusalem* – olivepresspublisher.com – p129, quoting "The Global Divide on Homosexuality", PewResearchCentre, June 4th 2013, http://www.pewglobal.org/2013/06/04/the-global-divide-on-homosexuality/
[3] Benjamin Pogrund, www.theguardian.com May 22 2015

CHAPTER 9 – BATTLE FOR TRUTH CONTINUES

Back to the question with which we began the previous chapter: *Is there really media bias against Israel in the West?* Let me quote from one of my favourite writers, Melanie Phillips. While acknowledging that it is not uncommon for issues to be misunderstood out of ignorance, laziness or indifference, the brilliant columnist writes: "What is unique about the treatment of Israel is that a conflict subjected to an unprecedented level of scrutiny should be presented in such a way as to drive out truth and rationality. History is turned on its head; facts and falsehoods, victims and victimizers are reversed; logic is suspended, and a fictional narrative now widely accepted as incontrovertible truth. This fundamental error has been spun into a global web of potentially catastrophic false conclusions. The fraught issue of Israel sits at the epicentre of the West's repudiation of reason. Many of the errors and misrepresentations about the Middle East conflict not only promote falsehood but turn the truth inside out... In Britain and much of Europe, the mainstream, dominant view among the educated classes is that Israel itself is intrinsically illegitimate.[1]

The narrative that Israel has been foisted onto Arab land is now accepted as true in the West. "But it is false," she asserts. Please read her book for a full treatment of this and other issues.

Take the hot potato involving successive wars with Gaza. A Canadian journalist claimed that the facts did not support the accepted story that a United Nations school was hit by Israeli shells. Writing for the *Canadian Globe and Mail*,

Patrick Martin investigated the shelling that led to the tragic deaths of 43 civilians. He reported: "Physical evidence and interviews with several eye-witnesses, including a teacher who was in the schoolyard at the time of the shelling, make it clear: While a few people were injured from shrapnel landing inside the white-and-blue-walled UN Relief and Works Agency (UNWRA) compound, no-one in the compound was killed. The 43 people who died in the incident were all outside, on the street, where all three mortar shells landed. Stories of one or more shells landing inside the schoolyard were inaccurate."

He added: "While the killing of 43 civilians on the street may itself be grounds for investigation, it falls short of the act of shooting into a schoolyard crowded with refuge-seekers."[2]

Martin's story confirms the under-reported accounts that the Israeli Defence Force accurately returned fire to the location from which it was being shelled by Hamas terrorists who were engaging in what Israeli Prime Minister Benjamin Netanyahu referred to as a double war crime – attacking Israeli civilians and hiding behind Palestinian civilians.

More unhelpful propaganda surrounded the boarding in 2010 of an aid flotilla trying to break Israel's blockade on Gaza (introduced for security reasons), which sparked off predictable fury from the world at large when it led to the killing of nine crew members. As in so many previous cases, the incident was widely portrayed in the media as the bullying IDF overpowering innocent victims who only wished to help ferry much-needed cargo to the stricken Gaza Strip.

But the reality was that the crew were at best naïve and more likely exercising a politically-correct belligerent attitude towards a nation who is even seeing its friends desert them. There is no question but that the Israelis came under fierce attack when they boarded the ship. Israel is not against such aid getting to Gaza – they are simply trying to ensure that it does not include arms destined to be used against them and it seems perfectly reasonable, therefore, that such ships should dock at Israeli ports.

As Malcolm Hedding of the International Christian Embassy in Jerusalem said: "Any fair-minded person, after viewing the IDF's video footage of the incident, will concede that Israeli commandos were definitely not boarding a ship-full of peaceful activists… for embedded among the passengers were a large number of well-armed militants." And in fact it later emerged that these 'activists' were radical Islamic jihadists fully prepared to sacrifice their lives, having left statements to this effect with families and friends. But the international community rushes to condemn Israel before the real facts have emerged.[3]

A few years ago, when the BBC hosted a discussion on growing anti-Semitism in Britain, it was interesting to note that even in the studio there was strong antipathy towards Israel. This became clear when everyone clapped at the mention of "what Israel is doing in Gaza", and yet no-one talks of what Gaza is doing to Israel.[4]

The former was a reference to charges of 'war crimes' committed by Israel for apparently targeting civilians while also responding 'disproportionately' to constant attacks from Gaza simply because Israelis lost fewer men than their counterparts in the conflict. But it is rarely, if ever, mentioned that the IDF do something virtually unknown in warfare by dropping leaflets to residents warning of an impending attack to give them time to escape.

In this and other ways, media bias is sometimes evident from what is not reported. As a further example, whenever disasters occur around the world, Israel is often the first to offer help and expertise while, closer to home, doctors have been treating soldiers wounded across the border in Syria's civil war.

Australia's born-again Prime Minister Scott Morrison has described as "intellectual fraud" the view generally put about at the UN of Israel being the centre of world cruelty when in fact it is a refuge from persecution and genocide boasting a free press, parliamentary democracy, financial prosperity and technological innovation.[5]

Something else rarely mentioned is the fact that Israel as a whole needs to restore their relationship with God, as they did in Jehoshaphat's day. They too have fallen into the ways of the world – with abortion and homosex rife, for example. Israel needs to repent and return to the God of their fathers who is (or should be) at the centre of their regular feasts.

Another fact greatly ignored, despite the cost to the British taxpayer, is the corruption on a grand scale practiced by the Palestinian Authority. Since the signing of the Oslo Accords, over a quarter-of-a-century ago, the Palestinians have received more than 25 times more aid per capita than the amount of money donated by the United States to Europe under the post-World War II Marshall Plan, which paid for the complete reconstruction and rehabilitation of the European economy. Put in simple terms, with the money donated to the PA over this time, we could have reconstructed the European economy 25 times! Even according to Arabic newspaper reports, PA leader Mahmoud Abbas receives a salary of one million euros per month – more than 30 times that of the US President![6]

All of which makes talk of Palestinians suffering economic oppression at the hands of Israel patent nonsense. At the end of the day we are witnessing a global battle for truth that is increasingly hard to come by in times of moral relativism when lying has become such a commonly accepted practice, particularly if it is to further a cause, as has been the case with Islam all along. Former PLO assassin Taysir 'Tass' Saada, who now follows Jesus and is a friend of Israel, has explained that "lying is viewed within Islam as an acceptable tactic if it advances the goals of the religion".[7]

The need for truth has never been greater and, as Tass Saada has discovered to his eternal joy, it can only ultimately be found in Jesus, the Jew, who said: *I am the way and the truth and the life; no-one comes to the Father except through me* (John 14.6).

[1] *The World Turned Upside Down*, Encounter Books.
[2] *Israel the Chosen*, Charles Gardner, CreateSpace (Amazon), p75.
[3] Ibid p77.
[4] Ibid p78.
[5] *Jerusalem News Service*, 25th February 2019
[6] *Peace in Jerusalem*, Charles Gardner, olivepresspublisher.com – p146.
[7] Ibid p104, quoting *Once an Arafat Man*, Tyndale Publishing, Tass Saada with Dean Merrill.

CHAPTER 10 – FULFILMENT OF THE FEASTS

Most people are aware that there is something of a crossover link between Judaism and Christianity – for example, that Passover usually falls around the same time as Easter. But there is much more to it than that. The truth is that Christianity is in fact a fulfilment, or completion, of Judaism – and all the main feasts celebrated by Jews for thousands of years have a direct relationship to what Christ has done in redeeming his people from their sins. They all point to the Messiah and are as relevant today as they ever were. Every aspect of each festival, described in detail in the Old Testament, has a perfect fulfilment in Yeshua, the Jewish Messiah, who also came to set the Gentiles free. I have already referred to Passover, but let us refresh ourselves with a brief look at the key feasts, and what they mean for Christians.

Jesus' first recorded miracle – at the wedding in Cana of Galilee – is the clearest example of how wine in particular played an important and indeed noble part in Jewish culture. Jesus not only blessed the couple with his gracious presence but, when the wine ran out – a great embarrassment for the hosts – he made sure the party continued by turning several huge jars of water into wine; and the very best wine at that, as the master of ceremonies pointed out in wonder. It is a shame that some Christians seem to have been turning wine into water ever since.

But our Lord was not just validating the drinking of alcohol or performing a party trick. He was declaring in no uncertain terms who he was. For on every Jewish Sabbath

(Shabbat), which starts of Friday sunset each week, the blessing of the wine at dinner is followed by the prayer of thanksgiving said by all present at the table: "Blessed are you, O Lord our God, King of the Universe, who created the fruit of the vine. Amen!" Our Jewish friends say it in Hebrew, thus: *Baruch atah Adonai Eloheinu, Melech Ha olam, borayprihagafen. Amen!*

By turning water into wine, Jesus demonstrated in the profoundest way possible that he was indeed God! Can you imagine the impact that must have made on those wedding guests who understood what he was effectively saying? As Aaron Eime, a Messianic Jewish leader in Jerusalem, points out: "He has just said, 'I am the King of the Universe'."

As for the Sabbath itself, it was designed as a time of rest from work when thoughts could be turned to family, faith and the fellowship involved in sharing food at the table in celebration of all God's goodness. It was given as one of the Ten Commandments but, though the Jewish people have largely kept this important ritual which has in turn helped to keep them together as a people, the Gentile world has effectively thrown out the principle with 24/7 shopping, working all hours and no time to stop and think about family, God or even our own health (which is severely affected when regular rest is not taken), not to mention what life is all about.

Actually, Jesus is our 'Sabbath rest' (Hebrews 4) – the epitome of the perfect rest and peace we can know who said: *Come to me, all who are weary and burdened, and I will give you rest* (Matthew 11.28). Jesus was the 'hope of Israel', as the Apostle Paul explained to the Jewish leaders in Rome where he was under house arrest. We are told: *From morning till evening he explained and declared to them the kingdom of God and tried to convince them about Jesus from the Law of Moses and from the Prophets* (Acts 28.23b). He was not making it up; this was no new religion, but a fulfilment of the old with which they were familiar.

Talking of Cana in Galilee, the town has a special place in my life, even though I have only seen it from a distant motorway. For it was there in the year 2000 that my wife Linda had a vision of her own wedding during her second trip to Israel. As she was representing her church on a tour involving Christians from Sheffield's Anglican diocese, she had been asked to pray for various members at appropriate points and so obviously marriage was an issue when she visited the church at Cana, where Jesus' miracle is reputed to have been performed. She duly lifted up the needs of couples who were going through difficulties. While she was watching some monks playing the guitar and singing praise songs to God, she suddenly had a vision of her own wedding, and could even see her groom, though his back was turned. This was a startling experience for a 43-year-old who had never even had a serious boyfriend, although she had been half-prepared for it by an earlier prophecy from Tracy Williamson, assistant to well-known blind singer Marilyn Baker, who was being hosted by her church and who told her that God was going to bring someone special into her life. Within five months of her Cana vision, we met on a blind date organised by mutual friends, and were married six months later.

Not many years later, Linda had a vivid and very powerful dream, and I soon knew all about it as she woke me up in the early hours of the morning.

"Charles, I've been with Jesus!" she gasped in a loud whisper (we were sleeping on our mobile blow-up bed in the lounge of her sister's family home where we were staying at the time and she obviously didn't want to wake up the children).

There was quite a bit more to her dream than I will share here, but a key aspect of it is particularly apt to our discussion of the feasts. She went on: "Although there were others there whom I knew, I was talking face to face with Jesus. He spoke about some members of the family, and how he had been there for them at special times of crisis in their lives without them even realising it.

"Anyway, he was very relaxed and I noticed he was drinking from a large tankard. I suppose I was expecting him to be drinking wine, or perhaps tea. And he must have realised what I was thinking and chuckled to himself before it became clear that he was actually drinking beer!

"After explaining that he didn't think much of the tea there anyway, he asked me a question, as of course Jewish rabbis are in the habit of doing: 'What does it say in the Scriptures?'

"And then I remembered what he said at the Last Supper: *I will not drink of this fruit of the vine from now on until that day when I drink it anew with you in my Father's kingdom* (Matthew 26.29).

"It was an amazing revelation." And we were so taken up with what had clearly been a divine encounter that it was some time before we drifted back to sleep.

The Last Supper was in fact the Passover feast that Jesus celebrated with his disciples before becoming the ultimate fulfilment of the festival – in God's perfect timing – when he took the punishment we deserved on the cross.

The feast was originally inaugurated to remind the Israelites how God had miraculously delivered them from bondage in Egypt. Pharaoh had repeatedly refused to let them go despite a series of plagues sent to punish his stubbornness but, when the tenth plague struck – killing the first-born of all who had not placed the blood of a sacrificial lamb on the doorpost of their houses – they were finally set free from their slavery. God had promised through Moses: *When I see the blood, I will pass over you* (Exodus 12.13). Some 1,500 years later, Jesus became the spotless 'Lamb of God', sacrificed for the sins of the world – and all who put their trust in his redeeming blood would be set free from bondage to sin and self and inherit eternal life. As one-time teenage pop star Helen Shapiro says: "Jesus was Jewish, and still is. When a Jewish person receives Jesus they are returning to the God of Abraham."

Shavuot (also known as the Feast of Weeks or Pentecost) falls 50 days after Passover, celebrates the first fruits of the harvest (wheat, barley, grapes, figs, pomegranates, olives and dates) and is fulfilled on the Day of Pentecost (50 days after Christ's crucifixion) with the birth of an explosive new era for God's people as 3,000 Jews respond to the outpouring of the Holy Spirit and the message of Peter that Jesus was the long-promised Messiah who had come to fulfil all their hopes and dreams. It was thus the first 'harvest' of souls for the kingdom of God under the New Covenant.

But Shavuot is also traditionally (as encouraged by the rabbis) the anniversary of the giving of the Law (Ten Commandments) to Moses on Mt Sinai and, on this level, is also perfectly fulfilled in Yeshua who came, not to abolish the Law and the Prophets, but to fulfil them, as he stated so clearly in the Sermon on the Mount (see Matthew 5.17). In fact, he had come to write the law on our hearts (see Ezekiel 36.26), not just on tablets of stone, to enable us the more easily to follow its precepts, as spelled out on the 'mount' (see Matthew chapters 5 to 7).

Sukkot, or the Feast of Tabernacles, is a celebration once again of the exodus from Egypt with specific emphasis on the 40 years in the Wilderness when they lived 'under the stars' and God protected them and provided for them in miraculous ways such as 'heavenly manna' and water from the rock. And so today Jews still mark this time by building temporary shelters out of palm branches and the like to remind them of God's provision and, indeed, their dependence on him –

and, I suppose, of the temporary nature of our lives on this planet in the light of the eternal significance of our souls and of God's kingdom.

It is also associated with the harvest (the full harvest resulting from the latter rains as opposed to the early spring rains) – a festival still widely marked in Christian communities. But there is also a deeper, spiritual significance as the Bible speaks of a latter-day 'harvest of the earth' when the sheep will be separated from the goats, when all men will have to give an account of what they have done and Jesus, the Judge of all mankind, will oversee the reaping of the good and bad crop as angels swing their sickles throughout the earth (see Revelation 14.14-20). It is partly for this reason that the Second Coming of Christ is widely expected to take place during the Feast of Tabernacles.

Amidst all the hatred poured out against Israel, God has not forgotten his people. Against the shameful background of blatant anti-Semitism at Britain's 2018 Labour Party Conference (September 2018, coinciding with Tabernacles), Jews everywhere were being reminded of where their help comes from. As tens of thousands descended on Jerusalem's Western Wall complex to receive the priestly Aaronic blessing during the Feast of Tabernacles, they heard afresh those solemn, soothing words of comfort: *The Lord bless you and keep you…* (Numbers 6.24).

But at Liverpool, home of *The Beatles*, some Labour delegates were not singing *All you need is love*, but joining in a chorus of hate-filled messages directed at the state of Israel, calling for an arms embargo and provocatively waving Palestinian flags. One prominent Member of Parliament stayed away altogether, and said she was glad she had done so when it emerged that Jewish MP Luciana Berger had to be accompanied to a conference rally by two police officers. And a colleague even warned that the anti-Semitism crisis could fuel the rise of Nazism in Britain. Walthamstow MP Stella Creasy told the rally: "Nazism doesn't turn up fully formed, wearing shiny black boots and black shirts and goose-stepping. It builds bit by bit, it gains little by little, it paints itself as the victim – it paints its victims as the enemies, as traitors, the 'other', with dual loyalty." [1]

But the seven-day Jewish Feast of Tabernacles reminds us that God, not politicians, will have the final say on Israel's future.He still promises to provide all their needs, especially in the face of fiery opposition. Psalm 27, traditionally recited during the feast and written by King David, notes: *When the wicked advance against me to devour (or slander) me, it is my enemies and my foes who will stumble and fall... for in the day of trouble he will keep me safe in his dwelling; he will hide me in the shelter of his sacred tent and set me high upon a rock... Do not turn me over to the desire of my foes, for false witnesses rise up against me, spouting malicious accusations* (Psalm 27.2, 5, 12).

The feast celebrates the time God came down to 'tabernacle', or live, amongst his people. And this is also what Jesus did some 1,500 years later when, as the Apostle John put it, *the word became flesh and dwelt* (literally *tabernacled) with us* (John 1.14). Jesus was also described as 'Emmanuel', meaning 'God with us' (see Isaiah 7.14, Matthew 1.23).

Jewish people believe that when Messiah comes, it will be during this feast. And there is good reason to believe that Jesus was actually born at this time of year, not at Christmas as is generally supposed. For one thing, the shepherds were in the fields watching their flocks by night – the lambs were still kept outdoors during the feast, but would have been kept indoors in winter. For another, Sukkot is a festival of joy – rabbis apparently teach that it is a sin to be miserable this week – and the angel announcing Messiah's birth said:

Fear not, for behold, I bring you good tidings of great joy... (Luke 2.10).

The feast also played a crucial role in Jesus' ministry, for it was on the last day of Tabernacles that he stood up to declare: *If any man is thirsty, let him come to me and drink. He who believes in me, as the Scripture has said, out of his inmost being shall flow rivers of living water* (John 7.37f).

The background to this is that, traditionally, on each day of the feast, the High Priest took a golden pitcher and filled it with water drawn from the Pool of Siloam, and it was poured out on the altar as a thank-offering for rain.

Jesus now promised a spiritual 'rain' that would never stop flowing for those who trusted him. And in the light of dark threats here in Britain, and elsewhere, consolation can surely be taken from the feast's association with the 'last days' when Jesus returns, once again to tabernacle with his people, after which all nations will be required to make an annual pilgrimage to Jerusalem in order to celebrate Tabernacles – and those who refuse to do so will be denied rain! (See Zech 14.16-19).

One school of thought teaches that when Jesus returns as King of kings, he will be hailed by the blast of the shofar (ram's horn) on the Feast of Trumpets (marked at the start of the autumn feasts) when all Israel would recognise him as Messiah and enter into national mourning over the One they have pierced (see Zech 12.10; see also 1 Corinthians 15.52, 1 Thessalonians 4.16). What a glorious prospect!

[1] *Daily Mail*, 24th September 2018.
I am also indebted for some insights to author and Hebraic teacher Fred Wright and to David Soakell of Christian Friends of Israel.

CHAPTER 11 – LIGHT IN THE DARKNESS

Each year as we approach the traditional season of Christmas, those of us who live in the Northern hemisphere are all too aware of the gathering gloom of midwinter, and are anxious to help dispel the darkness with a multiple array of bright lights. The prophet Isaiah addressed this contrast when he proclaimed that *the people walking in darkness have seen a great light* (Isa 9.2) – although he was thinking more of man's spiritual condition than their general environment.

Written around 600 years before Christ, this is one of his many references to the coming Messiah, and points (in the preceding verse) to the very region where he would engage in most of his earthly ministry – *Galilee of the nations (or Gentiles)*.

In the midst of the oppression of Roman occupation, a Jewish virgin would give birth to a son, who would be ascribed a series of majestic titles including 'Prince of Peace'.

Just as Christians do, Jews at this time of year also light up the darkness with a glittering host of candles to celebrate Hanukkah, the feast of Dedication.

I well remember sharing the excitement of the occasion with Jerusalem residents six years ago as joyful groups celebrated in restaurants festooned with brightly coloured lights and menorahs.

Though not among the prescribed seven feasts dating back to the time of Moses, Hanukkah is an eight-day Jewish festival Jesus himself attended and is celebrated close to Christmas (appropriately though not intentionally) to mark

God's miraculous intervention at the time of the reign of the ruthless Syrian-Greek emperor Antiochus Epiphanes who desecrated the Jewish Temple by sacrificing a pig there and blasphemously claiming divine status.

Judah Maccabee led a brave and successful revolt against the tyrant in 164 BC following the refusal of a Jewish priest to worship the Greek gods. This led to the re-establishment of temple worship (Hanukkah means 'Dedication') with the aid of the menorah (seven-branched candlestick) which burned miraculously for eight days despite having only enough oil for a day.

It was hugely important to Israel for the golden lampstand, or menorah, to burn continually. It was a requirement of the Scriptures instituted through Moses to indicate God's constant presence (light), first in the Tabernacle and later in the Temple (See Exodus 25.31-40 & Exodus 27.20f).

Indeed, the menorah has become the emblem of Israel, who are called to be a 'light to the nations' (see Isaiah 49.6).

Hanukkah – also known as Chanukah – represents the victory of the Word of God over pagan and anti-Semitic forces and is quite possibly a fulfilment of Zechariah 9.13: *I will rouse your sons, Zion, against your sons, Greece, and make you like a warrior's sword.* In Judah Maccabee's case, it was certainly a matter of the sons of Zion against the sons of Greece; little Israel up against a mighty empire.

Israel itself is a miracle! No other nation banished into exile has ever re-established itself and maintained its national language from time immemorial. The Nazis tried to destroy the Jewish people, but a reborn state of Israel rose out of the ashes of the Valley of Dry Bones (described in Ezekiel 37) – literally in one day (Isa 66.8). And the pioneers of the returned nation subsequently survived a succession of wars despite being overwhelmingly outnumbered by the surrounding nations attacking them, the most remarkable of these conflicts being the Six-Day War of 1967.

In Old Testament times Gideon defeated 30,000 Midianites with an army of just 300 men – only one per cent of the enemy's force. Modern aggressors like Iran and its terrorist proxies Hezbollah and Hamas stubbornly persist with their vain threat to wipe Israel off the map, but they are fighting against God.

In the autumn of 2018, when Hamas was raining down rockets on southern Israel, a bus was destroyed after taking a direct hit from a missile within minutes of 50 Israeli Defence Force soldiers getting off the vehicle. The Muslim Arab driver, who recognised that they would all have perished if the bomb had struck moments sooner, was reported as saying: "It's a miracle! God loves the Jews." And one of the soldiers said: "We began to sing the Chanukah song that speaks of the miracles that took place as God protected Israel." A YouTube video later showed soldiers dancing with joy at Jerusalem's Western Wall as they praised God for their deliverance.

In my opinion, the feast also foreshadows the coming of the Jewish Messiah Yeshua (Jesus), described as "the light of the world", and I'm sure it is no coincidence that it falls around the same time as Christmas (even though it is more likely that Jesus was born in the autumn) when much of the world is lit up with elaborate decorations to commemorate his birth some 2,000 years ago. Messianic Jews (who *do* believe Jesus is their Messiah) celebrate both feasts and it is interesting to note that the sight of a menorah as part of the festive decorations is increasingly common.

And yet at a time when billions of people celebrate the coming of light into the world in the person of Jesus Christ, a dark evil casts a shadow over the place of his birth as sabre-rattling surrounding nations threaten the very existence of Israel.

Paradoxically, the spectre of Armageddon (Hill of Megiddo), where the demonically-inspired kings of the earth will wage war on the forces of God at the end of history (see Rev 16.16), continues to loom each year just when the world focuses on the coming of the 'Prince of Peace'.

Armageddon is not some Sci-Fi invention of a film-maker's overactive imagination. It is a reality; for there will come a time, very possibly in the near future, when the nations of the earth will clash in a catastrophic battle on the plains of Megiddo in northern Israel – the Bible makes this clear. But then the Messiah will return in power and great glory to put an end to war and usher in a thousand-year reign of absolute peace. As my wife and I were reminded a few years ago in a Christmas card from the Jews for Jesus organisation, the baby born at Bethlehem is the only hope for peace in the Middle East.

Explaining the feast of Hanukkah, a Jews for Jesus spokeswoman said: "That is why each year we kindle our lamps, one light for each of the eight nights," adding: "The Hanukkah Menorah has nine branches and we light each of the branches with the ninth candle, the *shammas* or servant candle. The light of the menorah reminds us of our Messiah Jesus, the Servant King, of whom the Apostle John said: *The true light that gives light to every man was coming into the world* (John 1.9).

"We can't help but see the connection between the light of Hanukkah and the light that pierced the darkness when Yeshua (Jesus) was born. During Hanukkah and Christmas, let us remember that the light of the world has come among us to bring hope and life to all who believe."

But as Jesus was misunderstood, so are his followers. As John also wrote: *The light (of Christ) shines in the darkness, and the darkness has not understood (or overcome) it* (John 1.5).

Coming back to the UK after a lengthy tour of Israel in the autumn of 2017, we were particularly struck by the emphasis on Christmas – even our cappuccino at Heathrow had to be decorated with a tree-shaped sprinkling of chocolate! Christmas lights soon beamed on us from all sides, reflecting less on the theological aspect of the feast as on the usual glitz and glamour and commercial hype we have all come to know. And then there were massive crowds at the shops on Sunday – 'retail therapy' now being the new religion practised on what used to be the Christian Sabbath. Arriving on the outskirts of our hometown, Doncaster, we saw Christmas trees lavishly bedecked with baubles in a brilliant array of colours – and, as ever, we sensed the danger of not seeing the wood for the trees.

We are submerged in so much darkness these days – not least the marginalisation of the gospel to the point where it has become politically incorrect – and yet we all still make a huge fuss of this incredibly important Christian festival, celebrating the glorious truth of how God came to 'tabernacle' among us. However, the bright lights tend only to drag us further into the gloom of materialism, partying and pointless debt.

The context of the famous passage quoted at the beginning of this chapter is, most significantly, the darkness of the occult, which has gripped so many in our day. *When someone tells you to consult mediums and spiritists, who whisper and mutter, should not a people inquire of their God? Why consult the dead on behalf of the living?* (Isaiah 8.19). The prophet then speaks of a 'great light' that would shine among *the people walking in darkness*. No-one would be able to hold a candle to him!

Galilee, where most of Jesus' earthly ministry took place, was an international crossroads at the time, connecting Asia, Africa and Europe. Jesus performed many miracles there – in

Capernaum, Chorazin and Bethsaida, for example – warning those cities that they would be judged for their rejection of Messiah. Regarding Capernaum, he said: *Will you be lifted to the heavens? No, you will go down to Hades; for if the miracles that were performed in you had been performed in Sodom, it would have remained to this day* (Matthew 11.23).

Capernaum was destroyed by an earthquake in 749 AD. You can only view its ruins. Yet a short distance away is the town of Migdal, still a thriving community where former prostitute turned passionate believer Mary Magdalene came from.

But the light of Christ could not have burned without the oil of the Holy Spirit. As I was standing on the Mt of Olives back in 2017, I remember contemplating how Jesus paid such a heavy price for our salvation as he sweated blood among the olive trees in the Garden of Gethsemane below. The olive tree is a symbol of the Messiah. Its fruit is harvested using sticks to beat them down from the overhanging branches. Jesus was whipped for us! The olives are then crushed for their oil. Jesus was crushed for our iniquities (see Isaiah 53.5). The oil was then used to light a candle…to bring light to the world! However, not everyone accepted it, or understood it – because they loved darkness rather than light (see John 3.19).

Conflict over Jesus' claims was also apparent during the Hanukkah feast he attended. John writes: *Then came the Festival of Dedication at Jerusalem. It was winter, and Jesus was in the temple courts walking in Solomon's Colonnade. The Jews who were there gathered around him, saying: How long will you keep us in suspense? If you are the Messiah, tell us plainly. Jesus answered, I did tell you, but you do not believe…* (John 10.22-25).

It would seem that Jesus performed many miracles during Hanukkah, which is inferred from the discourse that follows, particularly verses 37 and 38 when he challenges his opponents to acknowledge the divine origin of his 'works'. In summary, Hanukkah celebrates the miracle that is Israel along with the light of the world – and miracle-worker – Jesus.

Millions of Christians today testify to being among those who once walked in darkness, but have since seen 'a great light'. Their testimony is the same as the slave ship captain turned hymn-writer John Newton, who so beautifully reflected the truths of the gospel with the words: "Amazing grace, how sweet the sound, that saved a wretch like me; I once was lost but now am found, was blind but now I see."

CHAPTER 12 – JEWS FOLLOW JESUS

Snake – symbol of healing and harm

Worshippers at Jerusalem's Western Wall were terrified when a large snake emerged through the cracks as they were praying quite recently. It is not a good idea to get too close to these reptiles until the time of the Millennial reign of the Prince of Peace when a *young child will put its hand into the viper's nest* and not be harmed (see Isaiah 11.8f).

Although the snake has the dubious honour of being depicted as Satan in the Bible, its status was somewhat redeemed into a symbol of healing as a result of God's instruction to Moses when the Israelites were dying of snakebite in the Wilderness. He was told to make a bronze serpent which, if victims focused on, would heal them from the poison (see Numbers 21.8f). This is still symbolised on the badges of the military medical services.

Many Israelites had died from snakebite as a result of a plague of venomous snakes sent among them by the Lord himself because they were complaining against God and Moses. In the event they subsequently acknowledged their sin and repented, causing the Lord to instruct Moses: *Make a snake and put it up on a pole; anyone who is bitten can look at it and live.* And that is just what happened.

This incident clearly foreshadowed what Jesus did for us all on the cross – that all who believe in him, who mark their hearts (or doorposts of their soul) with his atoning blood, will inherit eternal life.

Jesus told the believing Pharisee Nicodemus: *Just as Moses lifted up the snake in the wilderness, so the Son of*

Man must be lifted up, that everyone who believes may have eternal life in him (John 3.14).

It was through an explanation of this verse that Nick Howard, son of former Conservative Party leader Michael Howard, became a committed follower of Jesus. Nick had been impressed by the claims of Christianity at a meeting he attended in school, but didn't think it was for him because he was Jewish.

He had been very conscious of the suffering experienced by his family during the Holocaust, but it had not given him the answers to life's biggest questions. Then, at 15, he went along to a meeting organised by a Christian group where a visiting minister spoke on the gospel verse quoted above.

"It was explained that our rebellion against God was more serious than a lethal snakebite, but that Jesus was willingly nailed to the cross to solve that problem by taking the punishment for sin that we deserved. All we have to do is 'look and live'."

Nick was then reassured that being Jewish was no obstacle – far from it, in fact. "Jesus himself was Jewish!" the speaker explained. "He is the Jewish Messiah – the one the Jews were waiting for down the centuries. If you follow him, you will be following your own Messiah."

When Nick read Isaiah chapter 53, he was amazed to discover it was all about Jesus. A friend of his, who is also a Jewish believer, likes to say that Jesus fits the Old Testament prophecies about the Messiah like a finger fits its own fingerprint.

Now an Anglican minister in New York, Nick says: "In the light of all this, you might well ask why so few Jews believe in Jesus. One answer is the sad history of persecution by Christians, and another is because so few have heard that it is possible."

Isaiah 52.7 says: *How beautiful on the mountains are the*

feet of those who bring good news… who say to Zion, Your God reigns! We need more preachers who speak of this, Nick concludes. "May God raise up many others to tell Jewish people throughout the world to look with faith at Jesus, their Messiah, and live forever." [1]

As Nick discovered, the figurative serpent lifted up for all snakebite victims to be healed just by looking at it is a prophetic picture of the Messiah to come, Jesus, who would atone for the sin of all who put their trust in his blood. Indeed, he is also healer of body and soul, as another Isaiah 53 verse plainly tells us: *The punishment that brought us peace was on him, and by his wounds we are healed* (Isa 53.5b).

The Bible further tells us that there will come a day when *all Israel will be saved* in this way when they look upon *the one they have pierced* (Zech 12.10).

The devil wants to destroy Israel, but God will turn even the worst intentions of the enemy to good as the brothers of the Jewish Messiah recognise him as their Saviour (see Gen 45.4-8).

As it happens, the Palestine Viper has recently been recognised (by Israel's Society for the Protection of Nature and the Israel Nature and Parks Authority) as Israel's national snake, provoking the farcical, though not entirely surprising, response from the Palestinian Authority accusing the Jews of stealing their snake![2]

So now they are fighting over a snake. Someone is sure to get bitten.

---

[1] A fuller account of Nick's testimony can be found in my book, *A Nation Reborn*, published by Christian Publications International and also available from Amazon. And much of that account is taken, with his permission, from The Gospel Coalition's version of his story. See their website at www.thegospelcoalition.org

[2] *Jerusalem News Network*, 9th November 2018.

Escape from the Nazis

The annual Holocaust Memorial Day is held with the aim of ensuring that we do not repeat the terrible mistakes of the past, but I believe it is worth being reminded not only of how many perished, but also of those who escaped the jaws of Nazism – often miraculously.

It is a little known fact that in spite of terrible persecution in Eastern Europe, thousands of Jewish people were very open to the message of Jesus. In fact, research is currently being undertaken on the so-called 'Messianic' believers who died in the Shoah.

Among those who experienced miraculous deliverance from the death camps was Jakob Jocz, a Lithuanian-born third generation follower of Yeshua who became an evangelist to the Jews of Poland under the auspices of CMJ (the Church's Ministry among Jewish people), a British-based international society already reaping a plentiful harvest of souls throughout Europe and North Africa by the 1930s.

Such was the response to their work that the Warsaw branch CMJ chief Martin Parsons expressed the need for over 700 staff rather than the mere ten suggested at the time.

Jocz was sent to Birkenhead, near Liverpool, to train for Anglican ordination, and when he returned to Poland, he wrote: "In spite of anti-Semitism and increasing hatred, the Jews met us in many places with an open mind and with great readiness to hear the gospel." [1]

He added: "Today when the cross is being twisted into a swastika...Jewish men and women flock into the mission halls to hear and to learn about the wonderful Saviour."

In May 1939, he received an urgent call to England to replace the main speaker of the Church Missionary Society's annual summer conference, who was unavailable due to illness. In a recent research paper *The Rev Dr Jakob Jocz*, Dr Theresa Newell writes: "This was indeed a miraculous deliverance as members of his family died at the hands of the Nazis soon afterwards..." Jakob's father Bazyli was betrayed to the Gestapo and shot to death.

The family's story has something of a *Fiddler on the Roof* [2] ring to it. Jakob's grandfather, Johanan Don, was the local milkman in his shtetl (village) who first encountered the good news of Jesus when seeking medical help for his teenage daughter Hannah (Jakob's mother) who had been crippled in a fall.

The doctor was a Jewish believer and gave Johanan a Hebrew New Testament. He subsequently became a disciple, but died soon afterwards.

In order to make ends meet, his widow Sarah took in a boarder, a young rabbinic student named Bazyli Jocz. When he read Isaiah 53, he asked his teacher, 'Who is the prophet speaking about?' It was of course a situation very reminiscent of the Ethiopian eunuch's conversion in the Book of Acts (chapter 8). But the teacher was no evangelist, instead hitting him over the head and calling him a 'detestable Gentile' for asking such a 'foolish' question.

Bazyli was shocked, but undeterred, and after consulting the same doctor who had pointed Johanan in the right direction, he too became a believer.

He duly married Hannah, and Jakob was born in 1906. He became a noted evangelist and theologian whose writings represent a rich legacy of inspiration and encouragement for Christians – all called to preach the gospel to Jews.

As the Third Reich stormed across Europe, he wrote a booklet appealing to churches to speak out against the persecution of his people. As an Anglican bishop pointed out in the foreword, "he rightly calls attention to apathy in the church on the subject of missionary effort amongst the Jews."

Indeed, he challenged the church to become 'missional' as its *raison d'être* and to remember the call in that mission is *to the Jew first* (Romans 1.16).

If the church has no gospel for the Jews, he believed, it has no gospel for the world. He had total confidence in the authority of Scripture and stood on the premise that "loyalty to Jesus Christ is the ultimate test of the disciple," adding: "Commitment to Jesus Christ makes universalism (the idea that all roads lead to God) impossible."

He was highly critical of Rabbinic Judaism, lamenting that "making Torah into a religion robbed it of life" and saying that the removal of the sacrificial system (following the destruction of the Temple in AD 70) without their acceptance of the "once and for all times sacrifice" of Jesus led Judaism to a preoccupation with the study of the law. The irony of this, of course, is that the law was anchored in the fact that *without the shedding of blood there is no forgiveness of sin* (see Leviticus 17.11).

One of his theses was that the early church was much closer to the Old Testament than Rabbinic Judaism is today. And he advocated Jewish believers to fulfil the prophetic call to take the gospel to all nations.

Jakob certainly practised what he preached. It is estimated that, through outreach efforts like his, there were as many as 100,000 Jewish believers in Yeshua by the time war broke out in 1939, many of whom would no doubt have shared the fate of their brethren in the concentration camps but who would also no doubt have shared the life-giving gospel of their Saviour.[3]

[1] *The Rev Dr Jakob Jocz* (Olive Press Research Paper – obtainable from enquiries@cmj.org.uk) by Dr Theresa Newell, to whom I am greatly indebted for the basis of this testimony.
[2] The musical about Jewish survival amidst the oppression of early 20th century Tsarist Russia starring a poor milkman famously played by Topol.
[3] *Peace in Jerusalem* (olivepresspublisher.com) by Charles Gardner, p28.

A new spirit

Now in the 21st century, it is clear both from surveys conducted and media coverage along with the obvious numerical growth of Messianic believers that there is a new openness (secretly in many cases) in Israel to the claims of Jesus being the Jewish Messiah. He even became the focus of an award-winning Israeli movie, although it evidently failed at the box office. There is clearly still a stigma about being seen publicly acknowledging the 'Gentile' Saviour, especially in view of strong opposition from the Orthodox wing along with the risk of being disowned by one's own family. After all, the general perception among most Jews is still that Christianity is another religion altogether, and not the fulfilment of Judaism that biblically-literate Christians claim it to be.

A New Spirit, first shown at the Tel Aviv Cinematheque in December 2017, tells the story of former gangster Yaacov Damkani,[1] who fled to America where he was introduced to Yeshua as his Messiah and discipled in singer Keith Green's community. His life was turned completely upside down and, some five years ago, his testimony came to the attention of acclaimed film-maker Doron Eran while producing a documentary on the Messianic community.

Doron felt it had the makings of a Hollywood movie, as he shared with Shira Sorko-Ram (in the February 2018 *Maoz Israel Report*). He did not, however, anticipate the controversial nature of his subject – he has since been accused of being a missionary and betraying his people. He does admit to being a 'student' (of the New Testament) and the film's actors have clearly also been impacted.

Imri Biton, who plays the lead, responds to criticism

by saying: "Look what Yeshua did for Yaacov. He was a gangster. When he believed in Yeshua, he became a new person. These Messianic Jews are telling their own truth. As a professional actor, I can join them."

Doron believes the government has unwisely allowed the Haredim (Ultra-Orthodox) to take control of the nation's soul. "It is a religious dictatorship," he says. "They are brainwashing our nation."

He knew nothing of Yeshua before he met Yaacov. "I didn't know that He lived as a Jew and died as a Jew. I was told He was a Christian..."

Yes, it is tragic that both religious Jews and their Christian counterparts (by which I mean those whose profession is only outward rather than a living faith) have conspired to spread such misinformation.

Nevertheless, Jews are now responding in droves to hi-tech evangelistic efforts from within their own state, with an organisation called *One for Israel* (among others) reportedly making huge strides in reaching their people – their website is filled with testimonies of Jews who are now following Yeshua, and their various videos have attracted a staggering 55 million views, 15 million of them from Israelis.[2]

The inspiration for the movie, Yaacov's book *Lama Dafka Ani* (Why Me?), has been distributed free of charge to young Israeli tourists in New Zealand for the past 16 years as part of a programme called HIT (Hosting Israeli Travellers) which encourages Christians to host young Jewish tourists at little or no cost. HIT has now been extended to Australia and several other countries.

Many Old Testament prophecies speak of a twofold return of God's chosen race – first to the land and then to their Lord. The first stage, though far from complete, has been witnessed before the eyes of the world as exiled Jews from every corner of the globe have resettled in Israel, especially since the rebirth of the modern state 70 years ago.

The second stage began, significantly, around the time of the reunification of Jerusalem during the Six-Day War of 1967 as so-called Messianics recognised that Yeshua was indeed their Messiah and started meeting together in congregations all over the country. The movement has since grown substantially and they have made an impact on the nation out of all proportion to their still relatively low numbers.

Even some Arabs are recognising what is happening. Saleem Shalash, an Arab pastor in Jesus' hometown of Nazareth, is reported as saying: "The Bible says God will bring the tribes of Israel back together in this place, and suddenly revival will spring from here."[3]

Indeed, the small spring in the desert that bubbled up around 50 years ago is threatening to turn into a fast-flowing stream. The prophet Zechariah, quoting the Lord and speaking of things to come with respect to the Messiah's reign, wrote: *I will remove the sin of this land in a single day* (Zechariah 3.9). This suggests a sudden large-scale awakening.

Surely we are not far from that blessed day when they look upon the One they have pierced (see Zech 12.10) and welcome him back in the name of the Lord (see Matthew 23.39). Certainly, it seems that many have already looked upon Yeshua depicted on screen – whether online or at the movies. Perhaps a foretaste of greater things to come!

Many Jews like Yaacov are discovering that Jesus is their own, that he is not a 'Christian' as they were led to believe by rabbis and other religious leaders.

The Passover itself, which recalls the time when their enslaved ancestors were miraculously rescued from Egypt, was a perfect picture of what their Messiah would do for them one day. They were instructed to daub the lintels and doorframes of their houses with the blood of a sacrificial lamb, as a result of which the angel of death 'passed over' their homes, but did not spare the first-born sons of Egypt.

Jesus died on a cross outside Jerusalem as God's sacrificial Lamb and, if we mark his blood on the doorposts of our lives, we will find true freedom. As Moses led the Israelites through the Red Sea, which parted so they could walk through as on dry land, so Jesus takes us through the waters of death into a resurrection life with him.

Baptism in fact depicts this death and resurrection experience as St Paul writes of being *buried with him (Christ) in baptism and raised with him through your faith in the power of God, who raised him from the dead* (Colossians 2.12).

Yaacov's testimony is one of the great signs of our times. When the Apostle Peter stood up on the Day of Pentecost to explain the strange manifestations taking place, he was effectively saying "this is that." What they were witnessing was the fulfilment of Joel's prophecy, that *In the last days, God says, I will pour out my Spirit on all people...* (see Acts 2.17).

In the same way today, Christians are announcing to the world that the testimony of Yaacov and many other Jews represents the fulfilment of biblical prophecies, which speak first of the return to their ancient land of Jews dispersed throughout the globe for nearly 2,000 years, and then of their restoration to the Lord God of Israel, revealed in the flesh as YeshuaHaMashiach (Jesus Christ).

For example, Ezekiel writes: *I will gather you from all the nations and bring you back into your own land...* and *I will give you a new heart and put a new spirit in you...* (Ezek 36.24-26).

Jews have now been back in their ancient land for 70-plus years, which is very significant because it was the same

length of time they were exiled in Babylon from 586 BC
– long before their worldwide dispersion. For it was after
they returned from Babylon that they rebuilt the walls of
Jerusalem and re-dedicated themselves to the Lord.

The Bible also indicates that when the Jews return to
the Lord, the Lord will return to the world! (See Zechariah
chapters 12-14.)

Come, Lord Jesus!

[1] Sadly, Yaacov is today confined to a wheelchair, unable to speak or walk
after suffering a major heart disease. But in an update reported by *Israel
Today* on November 19 2019, his wife Elisheva said: "We are doing what
we can to bring the gospel to the individuals and many friends we have
made throughout the years."
[2] This figure includes only Facebook and YouTube views, not TV, etc.
(Source: *One for Israel.*)
[3] *Israel Today* magazine, December 2017.

Motorcycle encounter

I awoke one Monday morning to the sound of my wife's mobile phone bringing us more news from friends in South Africa, who keep us up to date on what the Lord is doing there – and elsewhere.

This time it came in the form of a YouTube link which really made my day. It was the testimony of a young Jewish woman from Israel who was abused as a child and later almost drowned herself in alcohol to ease the pain of her struggles, eventually contemplating suicide as she rode her motorbike, praying to God: "I don't want to live anymore; I want you to take my life."

At that moment she was suddenly enveloped by what she could only put down to a divine presence of love and hope running through her body from head to toe. She knew it was God, and desperately wanted to know more. So she sought out all kinds of 'spiritual enlightenment' including Buddhism and fortune-tellers, but to no avail. None of these was the source of her overwhelming experience of the warmth of God's love.

After a year of searching, she picked up a newspaper and read of an invitation to volunteer on a farm where free accommodation would be provided. She duly signed up and discovered it was run by believers in Yeshua (Jesus), and it was there that she came to know the living God who had saved her life on that motorbike. "I know that Yeshua is alive," she says with total confidence and assurance.

The beauty and wonder of the relationship she now has with Jesus was expressed in every syllable she uttered as she simply glowed with joy and delight at the new life she is now living and passionately sharing with others. (See https://youtu.be/f1-KBAWKk_g)

This is the sort of thing I was trying to convey to a gathering in London recently – that Jews everywhere are sharing their faith in Jesus, their Messiah, and that this is a sign of His soon return.

It also shows why Paul says that he is not ashamed of the gospel *because it is the power of God that brings salvation to everyone who believes: first to the Jew, then to the Gentile* (Romans 1.16).

It was the Jews who first brought us the gospel. Endued with Holy Spirit power received on the Day of Pentecost, Jewish evangelists took the message of Jesus throughout the known world, causing it to spread like wildfire – even under severe persecution.

That is why the Bible places such importance on Gentiles reaching the Jews for Jesus (see also Romans 10.1) – not only because it is pay-back time (i.e. we owe it to them – see Rom 15.27), but also because when they get it, they really do something with it! When they experience an encounter with God through his Son Jesus, they don't dig a hole and turn it into a memorial; they run with it – just like our young lady.

That is why, despite their still relatively low numbers in Israel, they are forcing both government and media to sit up and take notice.

Yes, I am well aware that Israelis on the whole are not yet fully following the Lord as a nation, but there is already a Gideon's army of passionate believers bursting with energy as they invest their time and resources into spreading the gospel. We should be cheering them on, and praying for them.

For if their rejection (i.e. Jesus' death) *brought reconciliation to the world, what will their acceptance be but life from the dead?* (Rom 11.15) … *If their transgression means riches for the world, and their loss means riches for the Gentiles, how much greater riches will their full inclusion bring!*

Not only are they God's "treasured possession" (Psalm 135.4), but they are also potentially the church's richest resource!

Lightning fails to strike

The scene switches from Israel to the southern shores of England where, in Bournemouth, Dorset, Orthodox Jew David Rose is now a passionate follower of Jesus.

It all started when he met a believer through Facebook. Family and friends turned on him, and he was barred from attending his synagogue, but he nevertheless rejoices in a personal relationship with the living God for the first time in his life.

He has since married his Facebook friend Christine, and also been baptized, both in the same church and in the traditional Jewish way – underneath a chuppah (canopy) for their wedding and in the form of a mikvah (a ritual bath taken before entering the Temple) for his baptism.

From the tribe of Levi, who are set apart for holy service to God, David (whose Hebrew name is Dovid Yonah ben Moshe Halevi) was nurtured in a North-West London Jewish community, observing the rituals and feasts and regularly attending synagogue.

It was through a Facebook group he joined in 2015 that he eventually met Christine the following year when David was struggling with his Jewish faith and its demands. He very much wanted to do something for God, and felt he should move to Bournemouth.

"As well as questioning my beliefs, I was into a lot of bad and ungodly things, which I knew were not pleasing to God," he explained.

Christine, meanwhile, told him she was a born-again Christian who had invited Jesus into her life some 30 years earlier and David became jealous of her apparent direct communication with God.

According to the Scriptures (Romans 11.11 & Romans 10.19 quoting Deuteronomy 32.21), this is something Jews will experience on meeting Gentile believers with a confident faith.

"I thought it should be me, a Jew from the priestly tribe of Levi, who should be having this connection with God. So I told her that I too wanted whatever it was that she had."

So her son Richard, a church elder, prayed with him and he was put in touch with Rev Ralph Goldenberg, a fellow Jew and retired Church of England vicar.

He subsequently attended a Christmas Eve service (which, in 2016, happened to coincide with the Jewish festival of Chanukah) at St Mary's, Ferndown, where Ralph was once churchwarden. "I was nervous because I had been told all my life that if I went into a church I would be struck down by lightning. And I was also worried about what people might think of me wearing a kippah (skull cap). But I was welcomed wholeheartedly and one lady even wished me a 'Happy Hanukkah'.

"After taking communion, and being nudged by Christine not to drink all the wine (which is the Jewish custom for feasts), I returned to my seat and began to feel strange. Suddenly I felt a 'whoosh' of cool air go right through me – and I knew I had received the Holy Spirit!

"My life has since turned around. I have been delivered from demons, and have had dreams, visions and messages from Yeshua. God is taking me on a journey, and I have complete faith and confidence in him.

"But because of my new-found faith, I am no longer welcome at the synagogue I was attending. Worse still, three of my children will have nothing further to do with me and old friends have also disowned me.But I know that Yeshua is the Son of God, and he has promised to be my support and strength."

David was baptized at St Mary's in October 2017 and returned to the church to marry Christine within a week. "That year was unbelievably eventful, and it turned my life around big time," he enthused.

Familiar as he is with the Jewish Tanakh, David has now discovered how it all points to the role of the coming Messiah, perfectly fulfilled in Yeshua. Among the many signs is the prophet Jonah, who was in the belly of a whale for three days and three nights before being spewed up on the beach. As with Jonah, Jesus died and was buried before being raised to life after three days. (See Luke 11.29-32.)

David now shares his new-found love for Yeshua, both within church congregations, which helps them better appreciate the roots of their faith, as well as with other Jews searching for the truth.

THE MISSING LINK

Forbidden book's path to peace and fulfilment

Almost 2,000 years after the Apostle Peter explained the Messiahship of Jesus to a large crowd gathered in Jerusalem for the Day of Pentecost, another David shares the same message with Israelis in Tel Aviv.

Also from an Orthodox Jewish background, this David was living the high life in America after serving in a combat unit with the IDF for three years and was making good money selling Dead Sea products while at the same time indulging in "all the pleasures the world had to offer". But it did not lead to real happiness. He knew there must be something deeper to life.

Then a Jewish customer asked him: "Have you ever felt God in your life?" It caused him to wonder if this was possible, so he started reading the Bible.

When he read in Psalm 22 the phrase *they pierce my hands and my feet* (verse 16), he wondered if it was referring to Jesus on the cross, which worried him because rabbis generally use the derogatory name Yeshu the Notzri (Jesus the Nazarene) with reference to Jesus.

So he did what any good Jewish boy would do. He called his mum, who scolded him, saying: "That's a Gentile book! We are forbidden to read it." She thought he was reading from the New Testament, but in fact it was from the Old (i.e. the Hebrew Bible).

His search continued until one day he came across a painting of Abraham offering Isaac as a sacrifice to God while, immediately above it, there was a picture of Jesus on the cross – God offering his Son as a sacrifice for us.

He got the connection and decided to follow Jesus (*Yeshua* in Hebrew) who, he soon realised, was not only Messiah but also God, a discovery triggered by the verse attributed to God in Isaiah 44.6 – *I am the first and the last* – which is repeated by Jesus in Revelation 1.17.

Unfortunately, all this coincided with tragedies in his family, and it was suggested that his new life may have contributed to their troubles. In any case, they felt he had betrayed his people.

But in time his parents noticed how much he had changed. "I was a typical Israeli 'punk'. You name it, I smoked it," he shared with the *Maoz Israel Report*.[1] With a warm but explosive temperament apparently common to those of Moroccan background, he was also tainted by swearing, pride and impatience, and had been addicted to smoking and drugs.

"Suddenly I wasn't doing any of that, and it didn't take long for my family to realise that these changes were not down to Yeshu the Notzri, but Yeshua the Jew.

"He came for all of us – first for the Jews and then for the rest of the world. It's just that we, the Jewish nation, rejected him when he came – just as we rejected many other prophets God sent. But there was always a remnant among the Jews who believed."

Now part of the Tiferet Yeshua Congregation, he can be seen on the streets of Tel Aviv sharing the message that turned his life around. "Yeshua was what I was missing my whole life. His peace changed my heart and transformed me for good. The more I learned, the more Yeshua won my heart and I just fell in love with Him."

"Now I feel called to bring the message of the Jewish Messiah to the people of Israel."

[1] David's story is abridged from the Maoz Israel Report February 2020, used with permission. For more details of their work, see: www.maozisrael.org

CHAPTER 13 – ARAB-JEWISH HARMONY

Christian envoy pays tribute to music teacher whose harmonica saved him from the Holocaust

The appointment of Israel's first ever Christian Arab ambassador is partly thanks to a Jewish musician who, alone among his family, survived the Holocaust. In a recorded speech following his installation as the Jewish state's top envoy to Muslim-majority Azerbaijan, George Deek paid tribute to the man he named only as Avraham who became his music teacher.[1]

It was because he played the harmonica so beautifully that his life was spared; a Nazi officer took him home to entertain his guests. When he finally found refuge in Israel, he chose to use the means of his rescue – his music – to bring hope to others including Arab children like George, who duly learnt both flute and clarinet.

George's moving story contradicts much of the narrative spewed out by the mainstream media about the Arab-Israeli conflict, especially the refugee crisis.

His family, who have lived in Jaffa (or Yafo) for 400 years, fled the city in 1948 in response to the warning from Arab leaders that Jews would turn on them when the new-born nation was attacked by the surrounding states, but that they would be free to return when Israel was defeated.

His grandfather, also George, had married in haste before fleeing to Lebanon, but when he realised that Israel had not been defeated and Arabs were not being persecuted, he managed to return and even got his electrician's job back from Jews he had befriended before independence.

While acknowledging that it was indeed disastrous for the 700,000+ Palestinians who subsequently became unwanted refugees, he noted that 800,000 Jews had been more or less forced out of Arab nations at the same time – a fact that is now conveniently forgotten.

The Jews were absorbed into Israel, but the Arabs were not accommodated in the same way by the very states whose leaders had persuaded them to leave, thus creating an ongoing UN-backed stalemate in which the refugees are being used as political pawns.

"The Palestinians are held captive by chains of resentment," he said.

By contrast, the Jews had responded to the tragedy of the Holocaust by securing their future. With respect to his music teacher, "he chose life, not death; hope rather than despair" and began teaching the very thing that saved his life to bring hope to others – especially amidst the tension that existed in Jaffa between Arabs and Jews.

Referring to the way in which Avraham spoke little and reluctantly of his tragic past, which he suggested was reflected by the general response of Jews to the Shoah, he said: "Only when they had secured their future did they allow themselves to look back at the past."

Under the shadow of that great tragedy, Jews were able to build a country that leads the world in many areas. At the same time Israeli Arabs are the most educated Arabs in the world, occupying highly influential positions as judges, doctors, MPs enjoying the right to criticise the government, and diplomats like him.

George is not Israel's first Arab ambassador – that distinction went to Ali Yahya, who was appointed Ambassador to Finland in 1995. And I have personally met Ishmael Khaldi – Israel's first Bedouin diplomat.

Towards the end of his speech, George quoted the words

of the Jewish patriarch Joseph, who reacted to the betrayal of his brothers in selling him to slavery by forgiving them and saying: *You intended to harm me, but God intended it for good to accomplish what is now being done, the saving of many lives* (Gen 50.20).

Joseph emerged as saviour of his people, rescuing them from famine after becoming Prime Minister of Egypt, and was a picture of the Messiah to come who would be nailed to a cross by his brothers but who would also one day reveal himself to them as *the one they have pierced* (Zech 12.10), forgiving and cleansing them of their past sins.

Like so many of his cousins, George might well have become a Palestinian refugee without rights or citizenship, but – through God's grace – he is an Israeli diplomat representing one of the most thriving economies on the planet.

I particularly like this story because of the crucial part played by the harmonica, an instrument I love to play myself and which can wonderfully enhance worship of God. I also like it because of its setting in Jaffa, known in Bible times as Joppa.

It was on our last trip to Israel that my wife Linda and I got to know the city, which lies at the southern end of the Tel Aviv metropolis. It was an awesome experience to discover afresh the vital role it had played in the biblical era. It is where the prophet Jonah caught a ship for Tarshish in his vain attempt to run away from God's call to preach to the cruel Ninevites – there is a life-size sculpture of a whale (complete with fountain) near the seafront.

Joppa was also a key location for the early church, and of another resurrection – Tabitha (or Dorcas) was raised from the dead there through the prayers of Peter (Acts 9.36-43). It was also the town of Simon the Tanner, in whose home Peter had the heavenly vision that was to open the way for the gospel to the Gentile world with his visit to the Roman centurion Cornelius some 40 miles up the coast in Caesarea (Acts 10).

It could hardly have been a more strategic place, leading to reconciliation at the cross for both Jew and Gentile. And now, 2,000 years later, an Arab Christian there finds hope – and status – in a Jewish world. Who would have thought a Jewish state would appoint a Christian envoy to a Muslim country! Pray for George. God is surely at work.

[1] *Christians United for Israel*, November 16th 2018

Something good from Nazareth

When the Israeli town of Nazareth is mentioned, most people immediately think of Jesus. It is where he came from. But when Nathanael, one of Christ's first disciples, heard that the Messiah was from Nazareth, he responded rather sceptically with the question: *Can anything good come from there?* (John 1.46).

The same question is sometimes asked today as the Galilean town is now an entirely Arab community with very few Christian believers. Step in the Sakhnini family. Although part of the town's minority Christian-Arab population, there was a time when being 'Christian' merely described their culture – it just meant that, unlike most of the Arab world, they were not Muslims.

That is until 2007 when Bishara, a barber and head of the family, was betrayed by a close friend – and soon afterwards received news that his sister-in-law was dying of cancer, with only a month to live. In the midst of it all, his wife Sarah was found to be expecting their fourth child.

A pastor from Haifa then befriended Bishara and began to share what the Bible teaches, especially about forgiveness. As a result, Bishara forgave his friend and received true forgiveness for his own sins. Not only that, but his whole family, including his three pre-teen sons, agreed to fast for three days as they prayed for their stricken relative, who subsequently walked out of hospital completely healed! And Sarah had a healthy baby soon afterwards despite an initial scare.

Having witnessed such miracles, including the power of fasting and forgiveness, the family's transformation sent shockwaves through the community. But they were scorned by their Arab neighbours, just as Jesus had been at the hands of the Jewish religious leaders.

And their world understanding was further rocked when some Jewish believers came to visit. They had not even realised Jesus was Jewish, let alone that an increasing number of Jews believed in him. Now they worship together with their Jewish brothers on a regular basis.

"Seeing us sing and dance together as we worship the same God," writes Shani Ferguson in *Maoz Israel's* monthly report, "was mesmerising to outsiders and always elicited questions."

She adds that "there is no greater testimony to unbelieving Jews that Yeshua has power over all than when Arabs embrace them as the people of their Saviour."

It is a little known fact that Arabs and Jews are meeting together at an increasing number of fellowships all over Israel, demonstrating the truth of the gospel that true peace and reconciliation can only be found through what Jesus has done on the cross.

The Apostle Paul wrote: *For he himself (Christ) is our peace, who has made the two groups (Jew and Gentile) one and has destroyed the barrier, the dividing wall of hostility* (Ephesians 2.14).

The Sakhnini brothers – Adeeb, Eliya and Yazid – are particularly skilled musicians and are now engaged on a project to reach the Arab world with a blend of Arab and Jewish sounds as part of the Israel Worship Initiative. They are currently working on a unique album, including some original and some old Arab hymns.

If you wish to help reach the Middle East with Arabic gospel songs, contact www.maozisrael.org or their UK branch at www.maozisrael.uk/

Maoz Israel Ministries is a non-profit organisation founded by Ari and Shira Sorko-Ram and dedicated to reaching

Israel with the good news of Jesus as well as providing humanitarian and other aid. Ari is a former film actor who has also played professional rugby and football. For more information on Arab-Jewish reconciliation, read my book *Peace in Jerusalem* (available from olivepresspublisher.com as well as from Amazon and Eden Books).

Investing in Israel

Now let us wind the clock back a little. When a young barrister came into a great fortune over 200 years ago, he did not spend it on himself but instead used it to turn the key that would eventually unlock the fulfilment of numerous biblical prophecies.

Lewis Way must have been dumbstruck when, for no obvious reason, he became the main beneficiary of a friend's Will, the only stipulation for which was that the money should be used "to the glory of God".[1]

The inheritance was worth £300,000 – a colossal amount at the time representing at least £12 million in today's money.

An Eton-educated 'mover and shaker' in influential circles, Lewis sought the Lord in prayer and duly felt the call of God to devote his time, energy and recently acquired wealth towards helping Jewish people to a knowledge of their Messiah and restoring them to the land of Israel.

He was particularly stirred by what has been dubbed his 'Exeter Road encounter' when, in 1811, he passed the home of two sisters who had also inherited a fortune and was reminded of how one of them was said to have planted a row of oak trees over which she had prophesied that they would stand until the Jews were back in Palestine.

"The spirit of that story really inspired him," Rev Alex Jacob told an audience in Nottinghamshire. "He knew at that moment that the return of the Jewish people to their ancestral home would be his chief cause for the rest of his life."

So he pursued this task with great zeal and became active with the Church's Ministry among Jewish people (CMJ), co-founded in 1809 by his close friend William Wilberforce and dedicated to investing in Israel's spiritual rebirth.

Unlike today, it was quite fashionable – even politically correct – to be linked with such an organisation, especially with the Duke of Kent (Queen Victoria's father) as patron... until he resigned because the mission was "too evangelical".

There was an irony, too, in that the Way family had in earlier years acquired their wealth through slavery, yet now he was teaming up with an abolitionist. Rev Jacob, CMJ's UK chief executive, explained that the Jewish emancipation and anti-slavery movements were two sides of the same coin. So when, in 1815, CMJ hit a financial crisis, Way stepped in with a significant gift, without which the society would have been a footnote in church history.

A great networker, he then set up a successful work in Poland, where many Jews came to believe Jesus as their Messiah. In 1817 he had an audience with Czar Alexander I of Russia, pleading with arguably the most powerful ruler of the time that the Jewish people should have their own homeland. And on October 13th the following year, with the Czar's backing, he put the case for the issue – and for Jewish emancipation[2] generally – to the European Congress.[3]

His meeting with the Czar is said to have significantly advanced the Jewish hope for returning to their ancient land and eventually led to the issuing by the British Government of the Balfour Declaration in 1917 which paved the way for the modern state of Israel.

Way was accompanied on this trip by an ex-Muslim Arab (his translator) and a former Jewish rabbi who embraced each other as they worked together in the cause of Christ and of Israel. The briefcase Way used for the occasion has survived to this day and was actually displayed alongside the podium at which Rev Jacob spoke at CMJ's UK headquarters.

Way and the Czar developed a bond as brothers in Christ and, after addressing the Congress, the Englishman wrote to his wife Mary: "Certainly, such an appeal for the Jewish people has not been made since the days of Mordecai and Esther."

There is no doubt that Way's sacrificial exploits greatly contributed to the cause of Zionism and the return to the Holy Land of Jews dispersed to every corner of the globe by the Romans almost 2,000 years ago.

His ultimate purpose, however, was not just in helping them back to their land but, more importantly, to their Lord. And he will have been thrilled to see the proliferation throughout Israel today – and in other parts of the world including the UK – of Jewish congregations worshipping Yeshua.

The bi-centenary of Way's presentation to the European Congress was marked with a special event at Stansted Park in Hampshire, once Way's family home. It was held in the historic St Paul's Chapel, situated within the Park, and addressed by Dr Richard Harvey, Rodney Curtis and Rev Jacob giving talks titled *From Russia with Love*, *The Forgotten Way* and *Money, Money, Money* respectively.

The chapel happens also to contain a unique stained glass window designed by Way while carrying out renovation work in 1804. It is the only window in a Christian place of worship which is wholly Jewish in design and symbolism. Recently restored with help from CMJ, this beautiful window is based on Genesis 9.13: *I have set my rainbow in the clouds, and it will be the sign of the covenant between me and the earth.*

Despite his immense earthly wealth, Way successfully stored up his treasure in heaven, as Jesus advises us to do (see Matthew 6.19-21).

[1] It is suggested that his benefactor and namesake John Way (no relative) would have been hugely impressed by his friend's integrity for, when he offered him an arranged marriage with a woman of high status, he turned it down, preferring to 'marry for love'.

[2] Jews throughout Europe had their rights restricted in many ways, such as being denied access to various professions.

[3] Set up following the collapse of the Napoleonic empire as a kind of precursor for the League of Nations in a bid to help re-shape the map of Europe.

CHAPTER 14 – A GENTILE PERSPECTIVE

General meets the risen Jesus

Now for something a little different – testimonies involving a reversal of roles. That is, Gentiles who have benefited from the Jewish Messiah, now officially numbered at 1.6 billion. But these next two accounts have a special link with Israel, as you will see.

We heard about the Roman centurion who was hugely blessed by his encounter with Christ, but here is the story of a senior British military officer who met Jesus in the very garden where he is reputed by some to have been buried 2,000 years ago.

Major-General Tim Cross (now retired) was converted after being struck by the reality of the risen Christ during a visit to Jerusalem over Easter. It changed him forever, and his Christian faith is now the driving force of his life. In an interview I conducted on behalf of New Life Publishing, the General recalled the dramatic encounter he had while on leave in Israel with his wife Christine during a peace-keeping post in Cyprus in 1981.

He was a captain at the time, having been raised in what he describes as "a typical middle class British home". He attended a Church of England primary school and, like most people, assumed he was a Christian. He even took the unusual step of being confirmed while at Sandhurst (the military academy), took communion during his wedding and had his three children christened (infant baptism).

So when the opportunity came for a short break in Israel

over the Easter weekend – celebrating the crucifixion and resurrection of Jesus, the heart of Christian beliefs – he and Christine hitched a ride on a United Nations plane and took in the sights of the Holy Land.

"I remember going past the bus station near the Damascus Gate (to the Old City) and noticing the hill behind it looking like a skull" (widely thought to be the location of Christ's crucifixion, referred to in the Bible as Golgotha – place of the skull).

"On Easter Sunday we visited the Church of the Holy Sepulchre (generally considered to have been built where Jesus was buried) and then attended a service at St George's (Anglican) Cathedral where it was suggested I visit the Garden Tomb, not far from the bus station.

"Our guide, a retired military officer called Colonel Orde Dobbie, showed us round and explained how this could equally have been the place where Jesus was buried. He read the Gospels and, most importantly, pointed out the empty tomb cut in the rocks on the edge of the garden. I sheepishly took his advice, and had a look inside.

"This is a pretty crucial issue, and I was really struck by the reality of the empty tomb. It was not a Damascus Road experience (like the Apostle Paul had when he fell off his horse on seeing the risen Christ); more of an Emmaus Road experience (when the risen Christ drew alongside two disciples who did not at first recognise him, but their eyes were opened when he broke bread with them). And it also happened to coincide with my 30th birthday!

"Back in Cyprus we had a very good Army padre, and within two months I was a committed Christian. Christine had meanwhile started attending a Bible study and committed her life to Christ independently of me. Everything changed from a personal point of view in the way I led and commanded. It has changed my view of the world and the way I saw myself in terms of servant leadership."

As to the relationship of faith to firearms, he admits to taking stock of whether it was appropriate to continue in the military – he had wanted to be a soldier since he was a boy. He prayed about it, spoke to others and looked at what the Gospels had to say, concluding that there was no biblical suggestion that you could not be a soldier and a follower of Jesus. John the Baptist, for example, told the soldiers to be content with their pay, not to leave the army. We need Christians everywhere, and the British Army – called to fight for justice and righteousness and be a force for good in an evil world – is a much more powerful institution as a result of that presence.

He added that the ethos of the Army is rooted in Christianity despite the increasing influence of secularism, and that it is definitely not an alien environment for Christians, with the ready availability of padres and the preponderance of church-related parades.[1]

He has also contended that, as a community, "the British Army recognizes the issue of spirituality, goodness, righteousness, justice, evil and wrong probably far more than most."[2]

In fact, devotion such as he has displayed since his conversion is clearly appreciated by superiors, many of whom are believers. While at Staff College in the late 1980s, his director of studies wrote of him: "This guy is a very committed Christian; he doesn't bash people over the heads with it – just lives it out."

The General added: "Faith had to be part of who I was, how I commanded, the way I spoke and the decisions I took."

This was especially the case during his third tour of the Balkans in 1999 – again over Easter. He was a Brigadier at the time, in charge of 5,000 men, and at the request of the UN became responsible for coordinating multi-national troops and civilian agencies in establishing refugee camps in the aftermath of the Kosovo War. "People were beginning to die, and had no food. As a Christian commander, I didn't hesitate."

His soldiers duly knuckled down to build the camps and he was made a Commander of the Order of the British Empire (CBE) for his role, meeting the Queen at the ceremony. But he says: "I just gave the orders. The men under my command did all the hard work."

His learning curve was further extended in the run-up to the invasion of Iraq in 2003 during which he tried to persuade Prime Minister Tony Blair to delay matters due to inadequate post-war planning. He was involved with others in planning the invasion and had spent some time in Washington from where he sent daily reports to government departments such as the Ministry of Defence and the Foreign Office.

He went to see Alastair Campbell (Mr Blair's right-hand man) "who was very helpful" and subsequently spoke to the PM himself, effectively telling him: "We're not ready for post-war Iraq."

That his advice was not heeded is well-known. The General did not take it personally, however, recognising that Mr Blair was getting lots of advice from all sides, and had to weigh it all up.

Testifying before the Iraq Inquiry in December 2009, he said he had urged Mr Blair and his aide, Mr Campbell, to delay the invasion two days prior to the start of the conflict. He further told inquiry chairman Sir John Chilcot that preparations for post-war Iraq were "woefully thin" and went on to say that "although I was confident that we could secure a military victory, I offered my view that we should not begin that campaign until we had a much more coherent post-war plan."[3]

Seven years on, he said: "I wasn't against the war in Iraq;

it was just not the right time. It did mean, however, that I was involved in failure for the first time in my life, which is something I am now able to share with others."

The greatest of Bible figures, such as King David and the Apostle Peter, also experienced this. "The issue is not failure, but how you respond to it."

Furthermore, there is a moral dimension to the army's purpose, which is just as important as your equipment and knowhow in terms of ability to deliver fighting power. "You've got to have people with a will to fight and the will to win."

In an interview with the Christian Broadcasting Network in 2009, he said: "If you lose the moral component, you lose everything. I think we – collectively in the West – have gone through 30-40 years of pretending that this is not important, and that I don't need to have a biblical foundation in my life. And I challenge that."

As to the argument over a nuclear deterrent, he said it worked during the Cold War and is still clearly needed. Russia remains a threat. And, yes, Islamic extremism is obviously a serious issue.

"We will not destroy Islamic extremism any more than destroy the idea of a united Ireland. But over and above that there are nations like Iran who don't like the West much; and a nuclear weapon in their hands could be a serious threat to us."

Does war ever solve anything? Well, the military remit is wider than shooting. As his career so clearly testifies, they have been involved in important peace-keeping and humanitarian operations. And the General describes their current role as "to try to establish a secure environment within which politicians can try to work out a solution".

"But we live in a fallen world marred by brutal dictatorships. And we are called to fight for justice and righteousness."

[1] Writing in the British Army Review, he described ideas of a secular army as 'tripe' and 'dangerously wrong', and removing reference to God in the Girl Guides' motto as 'vapid and anodyne'.
[2] Wikipedia
[3] Ibid.

A Precious Passing

I have not met the General in person – the above story is the result of an hour-long phone conversation – but my next witness was a special friend who, because of his great love for Israel, is thought to have literally saved many Jewish lives by supporting efforts to bring them to Israel from places where they were being severely persecuted.

They say death is the ultimate statistic – it will happen to us all. But there is a time to die, the Bible says (Ecclesiastes 3.2), and in the case of my dear friend Martin Hall, there was a sense in which it was perfectly timed amidst an atmosphere of profound beauty, sweetness, glory and triumph, although of course tinged with the bitterness of loss, especially for Margaret, his wife of 41 years.

I now understand what the Bible means when it says, *Precious in the sight of the Lord is the death of his faithful servants* (Psalm 116.15). As he struggled for breath in his last moments, you got the sense that he was about to breast the tape of a marathon of discipleship, serving Christ with such wholeheartedness and humility. And that he could say with St Paul: *I have fought the good fight; I have finished the race, I have kept the faith. Now there is in store for me the crown of righteousness, which the Lord, the righteous Judge, will award to me on that day – and not only to me, but also to all who have longed for his appearing* (2 Timothy 4.7f).

The sweetness of the occasion became even more appropriate when his funeral took place at Rosh Hashanah, the Jewish New Year, associated as always with apples and honey. There was never any pomp or circumstance about Martin's endeavours for the Lord; he was just happy to mingle unnoticed with the crowd of faithful 'joggers', striving for that special medal for all valiant finishers.

From a human perspective, you might easily have passed him off as just another runner in the field of gospel work, but you would have missed the unsung hero that he really was. Because he never blew his own trumpet, you would not have known, for example, that he had probably saved countless Jewish lives through his generosity and support, both in prayer and finance, of projects dedicated to rescuing Jews from anti-Semitic environments in Europe and beyond by providing them with the necessary documents and safe passage to Israel.

Dr Fred Wright, who is involved in this work, said at his funeral: "He would never let an opportunity go by without offering to help. In the last communication we had, he was asking how he could help Jewish people in Venezuela and Argentina. Martin was a great facilitator who embodied all the elements of what the Bible describes as a righteous man. The world is a sadder place for his absence and the kingdom has lost one of its greatest servants – a kind, gentle and humble man. Our loss is heaven's gain."

Martin loved the Jews because he loved Jesus, the Jew, and – though a smart high-flyer in the business world – he was sold out for the kingdom of God.

My wife Linda kept Margaret company during the long night leading up to his passing at the Doncaster Royal Infirmary. At one point she recalled a framed picture she had at home, by artist Lesley Hollingworth, of a beautiful gold-trimmed cup underscored with a verse from Isaiah 62.3: *You will be a crown of splendour in the Lord's hand, a royal diadem in the hand of your God.*

Linda picks up the story: "I went home to fetch it, removed it from its frame and tried to convey to Martin how God saw him that way: lots of bright colours, with the gold showing how precious and valuable he was. As soon as I finished, another friend, Ginnie White, joined me at his bedside –

Margaret had gone home to change at this stage. Ginnie heads up an international dance ministry and had come straight to the hospital from the airport following a tour of Northern Ireland as she had a special song she wanted to sing over Martin. I was simply amazed as I heard her singing about a cup of many colours which, wherever it had cracked, God had filled with gold!

"Ginnie's song; my picture," I told him. "Such perfect symmetry… We continued singing, worshipping and reading the Scriptures (they say that hearing is the last thing to go)."

Then, some hours later as the end drew near, Margaret began to share a powerful dream she had once had of being on the cross with Jesus and seeing this wonderful view of a beautiful landscape. And just as she got to the point where Jesus urged her, "Come and join me!" Martin took his last breath. He joined the Lord Jesus at that very moment, dying peacefully amidst the tangible presence of God.

Some 36 hours earlier, when he was still managing to speak, though with great difficulty, we deciphered that he was telling us (Linda and I) to be family for Margaret (who no longer has any immediate family). It reminded us of some of Jesus' last words – when he told John, his beloved disciple, to take his mother Mary as his own. It was a precious moment.

The haematology ward nurses, so caring and compassionate, were overcome with tears on his passing, especially on observing the couple's devotion to one another. Yet Margaret was able to console them with the words, "It's all about God's love!"

And so, as at Rosh Hashanah, it is not the end for him, but a new beginning. A celebration of his life was held at Bessacarr Evangelical Church in Doncaster not long afterwards on what would have been his 70th birthday. Ironically, he didn't want a fuss for his 70th, but he got one after all!

Most profoundly, Martin's lifetime has mirrored the blossoming of Israel foretold by Jesus (Matthew 24.32), having come into the world just weeks before international recognition of the re-born Jewish state by the United Nations and then watching it bud and grow into the powerful political entity we see today.

CHAPTER 15 – CHRISTIANS BACK ISRAEL

As whipped-up Palestinian rioters cried out for Jewish blood in their many recent days of rage against 'occupation' of their land, we should be praying that these dear people, for whom Christ died, would instead call on the blood of Jesus for their redemption.This is their only hope – and ours too for that matter. As Israel is tempted to quake in fear of the vicious international hatred being vented against them, may they too cry out for help from Elohim who sent his beloved Son to die as a sacrificial Lamb to atone for the sins of all who put their trust in him. The doorposts daubed in lamb's blood back in Egypt later became a wooden cross where God himself took the punishment we deserved.

In this battle over war and peace, the hordes of hell are being unleashed against the Anointed One and his people. But the Prince of Peace – not the diplomats or politicians – has the solution.

When believers the world over celebrated Pentecost (Shavuot) in 2018, I think it was highly significant that a *Jerusalem Post* writer credited evangelical Christians (or Christian Zionists as they are also known among Jews) for the current political breakthrough which has seen President Trump move the U.S. Embassy from Tel Aviv to the 'city of the Great King'.

"It is evangelical Christians who are standing with Israel today in ways that Nehemiah could never have dreamed about," wrote Tuly Weisz.

We are talking about their influence on the President as well as their love for the Jewish people who gave us Jesus and the Bible including almost the entire New Testament.

Weisz had asked Christian participants of a Jerusalem conference why the embassy move was so important to them. "The answer they gave is that it is foretold in the Bible," she wrote. Meanwhile Israel's then Education and Diaspora Affairs Minister Naftali Bennett said the move represented a new era in which the international community's relationship was based on reality and fact, not fantasy and fiction.[1]

I happen to know that the Mayor of Tel Aviv told an audience in his city that, without the help of the various Christian missions, Israel would not be where she is today. Bibi Netanyahu has said similar things of late about the value of Christian support for Israel.

It is worth noting that those 3,000 who joined the first disciples on the Day of Pentecost in response to Peter's sermon were Jews and proselytes from all over the known world (see Acts 2.5).

An indication of the significant role Gentiles would play in spreading the good news of Israel's God came with the healing of the centurion's servant at the start of Jesus' ministry. The Roman officer had humbly sought the Saviour's help, only requiring him to *say the word* as he felt unworthy to receive him into his home.

And so the gospel – to the Jew first (the leper who preceded this incident in Matthew 8) – was now also offered to the Gentile. We hear much about amazing grace, but Jesus was amazed by this military man's faith. The only other time he is recorded as having been amazed was by the lack of faith in his home town (see Mark 6.6).

I wonder too if our Lord was also prophesying of a day when faithful Gentiles would make an extraordinary mark on the world. In Yorkshire alone in recent centuries (I am biased because I live there) I can immediately think of three men who changed the world through their faith in Jesus –

William Wilberforce from Hull, a co-founder of the Church's Ministry among Jewish people who successfully campaigned for the abolition of slavery, Barnsley's Hudson Taylor, to whom millions of Chinese Christians owe their salvation, and Bradford plumber Smith Wigglesworth, who raised 14 people from the dead as he helped to pioneer the modern-day Pentecostal movement which had such a profound impact on twentieth century Christianity.

In honouring the Jewish people both in word and deed, we are simply building on the foundation laid by the apostles. But we must not forget the importance of prayer – after all, a ten-day prayer meeting had preceded that great initial outpouring of the Holy Spirit!

In terms of the recognition – and restoration – of Israel, the importance of prayer from men like Rees Howells and his Bible College students at Swansea in Wales cannot be underestimated. They had prayed many long hours at the time of the UN vote in 1947 before victory was secured.

In South Africa, although the present government stubbornly refuses to acknowledge Israel's right to defend itself, many Christians are on their knees praying for the peace of Jerusalem. Farmer friends from where I grew up emailed me in 2018, saying: "We are extremely excited with the USA's ambassadorial move to Jerusalem and continue to pray for this beautiful capital as well as for the region. What a privilege to witness what the prophets were only able to see in visions."

Those nations who oppose Jewish aspirations are in for a big shock. For they will come to nothing, as Isaiah predicted long ago (see Isa 60.12). Even the Boycott, Divestment and Sanctions campaign received a bloody nose with victory for Israel's entrant in the 2018 Eurovision Song Contest despite their efforts.

It is significant of course that the United States should take the lead in recognizing Jerusalem as Israel's capital, just as they had done back in 1948 when President Harry Truman was the first to recognise the new-born state. Apparently he took just eleven minutes to do so, but "later regretted that he waited so long", according to U.S. Ambassador to Israel David Friedman.[2]

In fact, there will come a time – perhaps in the not-too-distant future – when Jerusalem will become the capital of the world (see Zechariah 14.9 & 16).

Israel was blessed in 2018 with a royal visit from Prince William, second-in-line to the British throne. But at the Second Coming of Jesus, which is surely also not far off judging by the signs (see Matthew 24, Mark 13 & Luke 21), they will welcome the King of kings and Lord of lords (see Revelation 19.16).

Come, Lord Jesus!

[1] *Jerusalem News Network*, 16th May 2018, quoting the *Washington Post*
[2] *JNN*, 14th May 2018, quoting *Arutz-7*

Spurgeon – Can these bones live?

With respect to support for Israel from evangelical Christians, few could have been more vocal than the famous 19th century Baptist preacher Charles Haddon Spurgeon, who regularly drew thousands to his London church, the Metropolitan Tabernacle. He was one of several preachers of the day whose influence caused leading politicians to take up the cause of Jewish restoration to their ancient homeland, which led to the British Government's Balfour Declaration of 1917 promising to do just that.

In a sermon preached at the Tabernacle on Thursday evening, June 16th 1864, in aid of funds for the British Society for the Propagation of the Gospel among the Jews, Spurgeon took Ezekiel's vision of the Valley of Dry Bones as his text (chapter 37) and made it abundantly clear that the prophet was speaking about the restoration of the Jews both to their land and their Lord.

He conceded that some see this vision as a description of the resurrection, or of revival of a decayed church, and that although it could reasonably be applied to both, it was not the plain meaning of the passage. "He was talking about the people of Israel…" and the vision concerned them alone, for *these bones are the whole house of Israel* (verse 11).

"It was not a vision concerning all men, nor indeed concerning any men as to the resurrection of the dead, but it had a direct and special bearing upon the Jewish people. He was talking of his own people and, led by the Holy Spirit, he gives as an explanation of the vision – not 'Thus says the Lord, my dying church shall be restored,' but *I will bring my people out of their graves, and bring them into the land of Israel* (verse 12).

Bear in mind that, at the time, the land was part of the Muslim Ottoman Empire and it would be decades before Theodor Herzl inspired the Zionist movement that saw the beginning of Jews resettling there.

"The meaning of our text, as opened up by the context, is most evidently, if words mean anything, first, that there shall be a political restoration of the Jews to their own land and to their own nationality; and then, secondly, there is in the text, and in the context, a most plain declaration that there shall be a spiritual restoration – a conversion in fact of the tribes of Israel."

The tribes, he said, would be re-united and would serve one King, the Messiah descended from David, and "they are to have a national prosperity which shall make them famous...."

But as well as that, "the unseen but omnipotent Jehovah is to be worshipped in spirit and in truth by his ancient people..." (verse 14).

As to how it will all happen, he said it would come about through prophesying, first to the bones, and then to the four winds, as in the passage on which he was expounding – in other words, through preaching and prayer.

"It is the duty and the privilege of the Christian Church to preach the gospel to the Jew, and to every creature..." – to remind them of his love and promises, and to preach Christ crucified.

"After the prophet had prophesied to the bones (verse 4), he was to prophesy to the winds (verse 9)," praying for the Holy Spirit to *breathe upon these slain, that they may live*. And he adds: "There is no life-giving power in the gospel of itself apart from the Holy Spirit."

Not everyone will be involved in preaching, he granted, but all can join in prayer for the salvation of the Jewish people. "We cannot expect to see great things unless we cry to him; we are limited only by our prayers...O for greater faith, to believe that nations may be born in a day, that multitudes may be turned unto God at once..."

CHAPTER 16 – SIGN OF THE TIMES

In spite of the efforts of Spurgeon and others, the modern-day church is in danger of not recognising God's hand in Israel's restoration. As rockets and other explosives are rained upon Israel from enemies on their borders, anti-Semitic activity is also on the rise abroad. The Jewish people are under siege – both in their own land and around the world – and it is the duty of the church to come to their aid.

But this is clearly not happening as it should. For just as the Jews were punished with exile to the nations for not recognising the time of God's coming to them (Luke 19.44), the Gentile world (especially Christians) will be judged for not perceiving God's hand in bringing them back.

Israel and Jesus are among the major themes of the Bible, trusted by millions as God's authoritative Word. Much of it contains prophecy about things to come (at the time they were written) and, of these, top of the list are the frequent references to the coming of Messiah who would save his people from their sins and bring peace to people on earth.

But this would happen in two stages – he would appear first as the suffering servant and sacrifice for sins and a second time as King of kings and settler of all international disputes.

However, most Jews of Jesus' time failed to grasp God's two-part agenda and were looking only for a king to rescue them from Roman oppression. They overlooked the 'servant' aspect of his role so clearly foretold in the Scriptures (e.g. Isaiah 53, Psalm 22).

And yet, in fulfilling Scripture, he received a royal

welcome from the Palm Sunday crowd of disciples when they exclaimed: *Blessed is the king who comes in the name of the Lord!* (Luke 19.38, Psalm 118.26).

But in the midst of all this adulation, he was not taken in. He knew the fickleness of humanity and wept over Jerusalem, saying: *If you had only known this day what would bring you peace…* (Luke 19.42).

He went on to prophesy the destruction of the city and the massacre of its inhabitants (which took place within a generation), adding: *They will not leave one stone on another, because you did not recognise the time of God's coming to you* (Luke 19.44).

But the good news for God's chosen people is that he is not finished with them. For Jesus also prophesies the welcome he will receive from his people on his return when he says: *You will not see me again until you say, Blessed is he who comes in the name of the Lord* (Matthew 23.39).

But before that, just as a loving father disciplines his son, he will make good on his promise that, if his people forsake him, they will feel the sting of his severe reprimand (see Deuteronomy 8.5, 20).

Which brings me to the second most frequent tranche of prophecies in the Bible – those relating to the restoration of Jews dispersed throughout the nations to their ancient homeland.

For example, Ezekiel (speaking for God) writes: *For I will take you out of the nations; I will gather you from all the countries and bring you back into your own land* (Ezek 36.24). And he adds: *I will give you a new heart… and I will put my Spirit in you and move you to follow my decrees and be careful to keep my laws* (v26f).

We have just seen how, in focusing on chapter 37 of Ezekiel, Charles Spurgeon also emphasised these truths. And Jeremiah confirms this, referring to a new covenant

God will make with the people of Israel when he would *put my law in their minds and write it on their hearts* (Jer 31.31-33). And he adds that their restoration to Israel – *out of the land of the north and out of all the countries where he had banished them* – will be seen as a greater miracle than the crossing of the Red Sea (see Jer 23.7f).

I believe the watching world's involvement (or lack of it) in this great miracle prophesied so prolifically in the Scriptures is a litmus test as to whether they are for or against the purposes of God. This is borne out by Jesus' teaching, in the section of Scriptures addressing the last days, on the sheep and the goats.

According to theologian Frank Booth, his hearers would have linked this with Ezekiel's reference to judgment among God's own flock (Ezek 34.17) as well as to Joel's reference to judgment of the nations for what they have done to his inheritance, Israel, *because they scattered my people among the nations and divided up my land* (Joel 3.2).

Well, the nations have been busy dividing up the land of Israel for the past 100 years, ever since Britain was given the mandate to prepare the Jewish people for statehood. Not content with having lopped off 78% of the territory originally earmarked for the Jews at the Treaty of San Remo in 1920, the nations are still demanding that further so-called Palestinian land be conceded.

But the flock of God (those who claim to follow the Chief Shepherd) will also be answerable for how they either helped or hindered Jewish restoration – both physically (to the Land) and spiritually (to the Lord).

So we see that, in Matthew's Gospel (chapter 25), Jesus warns that many in the church will not be ready for his return (see the parable of the ten virgins), others will not use the revelation they have been given (the talents) and this will be summed up by their attitude to Israel (the sheep and the goats).

Where has the church been while this amazing miracle (of Jewish restoration) has been enacted before the eyes of the world, particularly over the past 70 years since Israel's rebirth? Have they been prayerfully, financially and spiritually supportive? Have they regarded the least of Jesus' brethren with compassion? Have they considered the enormous debt we owe them as recipients of the gospel that has set us free? (Romans 15.27). Have they prayed for the peace of Jerusalem, as the Scriptures command us to do? (Psalm 122.6).

Booth writes: "We are now in the middle of the second biggest prophetic event in history, yet sadly too many in the Church seem unable or unwilling to recognise it." And he adds: "If, 2,000 years ago, Israel missed out by being unable to recognise what God was doing in their generation, the Church is in exactly the same danger today."

Israel is not a peripheral matter for the church, something only for 'Christian Zionists' to get excited about. Tragically, too many preachers see it as a 'political hot potato' and so avoid it like the plague in order not to rock the boat. But this is a dereliction of their duty as servants of Christ. As with the mark of the Beast (see Rev 14.9-11), neutrality is not an option on this issue.

Jewish restoration is the great sign to the Gentile world of Jesus' soon return (Isa 49.22). And I will let Frank Booth have the final word on this point: "The return of Israel to the Land is the biggest prophetic event since the coming of Messiah; it loudly and clearly heralds his return, but many in the Church are not listening."

I am greatly indebted to Frank Booth for his insights in *Who are the sheep and the goats?* – an Olive Press Research Paper published in 2018. For further details, contact the Church's Ministry among the Jewish people (CMJ) on 01623 883960 or connect with their website at www.cmj.org.uk

When the fig tree blossoms

While spending time in north London looking after my mum (who is sadly no longer with us), I was inspired by the verdant overhanging fig tree almost blocking my path as I walked (and ran) around Hampstead.

Laden with ripening fruit, it was another reminder of one of the most significant events of our time, largely missed by most people – including Christians. For in speaking to his disciples about Israel's restoration and of his coming back to reign on earth, Jesus indicated that one of the signs of his imminent return would be *when the fig tree buds…* (Matthew 24.32f). The fig tree is widely understood to be biblically symbolic of Israel.[1]

There is much talk in church circles these days of a coming revival of fervent Christianity. There is certainly a need for one, and I pray it will happen. In fact, my understanding is that, along with much trouble and strife, there will be revival in the last days because Joel prophesied of how the Spirit would be poured out on all flesh (Joel 2.28). That was partly fulfilled at Pentecost of course, but its final fulfilment is yet to come, although Asia, Africa, the Far East and South America have already witnessed great outpourings of heavenly rain in recent decades.

But who in the church is preparing for the great revival prophesied for Israel? God has not forgotten them, nor has he replaced them with the church as some suggest. He has made an everlasting covenant with Israel – with Abraham, Isaac, Jacob and their descendants. Covenants are not meant to be broken; a disciple of Christ who expects God to go back on his word has completely misunderstood his character! If Israel is cut off from God because of unfaithfulness, what chance has the church with all her backsliding over the centuries – especially in terms of persecution of the Jewish people?

No, God will never reject his chosen ones. *Only if the heavens above can be measured and the foundations of the earth below be searched out will I reject all the descendants of Israel because of all they have done, declares the Lord* (Jer 31.37).

Even the New Covenant spoken of by Jeremiah is not addressed particularly to the church, as you might think from the context in which it is used over Christmas. No, it is with Israel that the Lord promised a new covenant, when he will put his law in their minds and write it on their hearts – and they will all know him (see Jer 31.31-34).

Earlier in the same chapter, he declares his "everlasting love" for his chosen people whom he vows to restore – to their land, which would once more become fruitful, and to their Lord, who says: *I will turn their mourning into gladness; I will give them comfort and joy instead of sorrow* (Jer 31.13).

If only the church would take a closer look at Israel, they would be so much better informed and live with much greater hope, for the Jewish state is a mighty testament to our God's great faithfulness and love. He entrusted the Jews with his word so that they could be a light to the Gentiles (see Isa 49.6), but they broke his covenant, forsook his laws and turned to idols instead.

Yet, just as the prophet Hosea kept faith with his adulterous wife, he has never stopped loving them. He is bringing them back to the Promised Land from every corner of the globe in perfect fulfilment of his word. Now almost half of world Jewry lives in re-born Israel, and more keep coming as anti-Semitism rears its ugly head once more in the nations to which they were dispersed for so long.

The Lord did not wait until they put things right. He honoured his promise and now waits patiently for the time when *they will all know me, from the least of them to the greatest* (Jer 31.34).

As St Paul put it, the day will come when *all Israel shall be saved* (Romans 11.26), echoing the word of Zechariah speaking of the time when they will look on him whom they have pierced and mourn for him as for an only child (see Zech 12.10).

Perhaps you look at the thousands who have marched through the streets of Tel Aviv in support of Gay Pride, or the fact that most of Israel's population are secular in outlook. But don't be blinded by that. See how the fig tree is 'blossoming': a nation has been rebuilt from a barren wasteland, now supplying the world with fruit, and a global leader in technology, using their agricultural genius to help African and other countries, and even using their medical expertise to heal their 'enemies' as they tend to the wounds of Syrian soldiers injured in the civil war that has been raging on their northern border.

But the real clue to their coming restoration is evidenced by the growing number of Messianic Jews – those who have recognised that Jesus is indeed their Messiah. Despite the high price paid by Jewish believers in Jesus (being cut off from their families in many cases), they keep 'coming home', like the Prodigal Son – not only in Israel but throughout the world. Yet the fig tree is still only in bud. But it will soon be laden with fruit, like the one in Hampstead's Spring Path.

The church really does need to 'watch' Israel, especially the growth of Messianic Judaism, for it is key to the unfolding events leading up to the second coming of Christ. It is also key to understanding the lovingkindness, forbearance and longsuffering of our God, who watches over his word to see it fulfilled (see Jer 1.12).

Sadly, many Christians cannot see what Israel has to do with them; they seem to forget they worship the God of Israel, which means in fact that it has everything to do with them. But if they only knew, for example, how Jews and Arabs are being reconciled through the cross (in accordance with Ephesians 2.14) and are worshipping together in many parts of Israel, their faith would be encouraged no end. For this surely underscores the truth that Jesus holds the answer to world peace.

Even on the war front, there are lessons to be learnt. The ongoing tension on the Temple Mount, for instance, needs to be understood more as a spiritual battle than a political conflict, representing on a grand scale what Christians are taught to expect in their individual lives.

Ignorance of Israel will leave your faith weakened while knowledge of Israel, even in its present largely unrepentant state, will edify your soul as you realise afresh that you can trust in the one and only Saviour of the world, for whom the Jewish people remain the apple of his eye (see Deut 32.10, Zech 2.8).

Some date the budding of the fig tree (metaphorically speaking) from the year 1967, a little over fifty years ago, when Israel recaptured the Old City of Jerusalem for the first time in 2,000 years, thereby ending (in the understanding of some) the 'trampling on' of Jerusalem by the Gentiles spoken of by our Lord (see Luke 21.24).

It is an interesting point that 1967 is generally also regarded as the year the modern Messianic movement began in earnest, coinciding (as it happens) with the breakthrough of the Charismatic movement that brought a restoration of the gifts of the Holy Spirit to the old historic churches.

The feast of Pentecost (known to Jews as Shavuot) is still seen in Israel as a celebration of the Law received by Moses, which of course is now 'written on our hearts' through the work of the Spirit in accordance with Ezekiel 36.26f. It seems that there is a 'golden' thread holding together this Trinitarian truth. So why not make sure that 'Jerusalem the Golden' lightens up your understanding of the Scriptures and of God's wonderful – though sometimes mysterious – ways.

[1] Dr Clifford Denton goes a step further and interprets the budding of the fig tree as a restoration in Israel of the authority to interpret Torah. See, for example: http://prophecytoday.uk/study/teaching-articles/item/661-being-hebraic-v-authority-to-interpret-torah.html

The God of Israel rules

More than 70 years since their discovery, the so-called Dead Sea Scrolls still back up the Bible's divine authorship. I will come back to this shortly.

Meanwhile threats from dictatorships like those in North Korea are frightening indeed, and could well ignite a nuclear war, but they are part of a bigger picture of worldwide rebellion against the God of creation. On a more specific front, they are a smokescreen for a potential Armageddon in the Middle East as Russian-backed Iran and its allies move dangerously close to Israel's borders.

Back in September 2017, Israel carried out a daring air strike against an Iranian-run weapons factory in the heart of Syria, severely damaging (if not destroying) the facility where chemical and biological munitions as well as medium-range missiles are being developed.[1] Syria in turn warned about "dangerous repercussions".[2]

The strike took place exactly ten years after Israel – the only country in recent years that had (until then) stood up to North Korea – destroyed a Syrian nuclear reactor being built with the help of the rogue regime.

British politicians, while appalled by the antics of Kim Jong-un, are nevertheless shaking their fists at God in their own way as, with their atheist agenda, they question the existence of a divine order. Like the serpent in the Garden of Eden, they pose the subtle question: "Did God really create man and woman to procreate?" (See Genesis 3.1.)

At the centre of the earth today stands a small Jewish state. And what the world interprets as an ideological battle over a piece of land the size of Wales is in effect an Arab-Muslim challenge to the God of Israel, revealed to us through his Son Jesus Christ.

Their claim that the land does not belong to the Jews despite thousands of years of historical, archaeological and biblical evidence was decisively countered by the 1947 discovery on the shores of the Dead Sea of ancient scrolls proving Jewish connection to the territory well before the emergence of Islam – and recognised as such by the United Nations that same year.

The findings in caves at Qumran included the entire original text of the Book of Isaiah, over 2,500 years old. This was found intact among hundreds of parchment scrolls hidden in the desert cliffs[3] exactly as it is recorded in modern times – no Chinese whispers here, but God's authentic hand. There is no doubt that the unearthing of these scrolls – along with much more archaeological evidence – fully vindicated Israel's claim to the land, quite apart from other political and biblical factors.

At the heart of all the sabre-rattling going on now is a battle – not really over whether there is a God, but over *who* he is. And the Judeo-Christian position that formed the basis of Western civilisation is that *He* is the God of Israel. When Sennacherib, the Assyrian king, threatened Jerusalem with destruction in ancient times (2 Kings 18 & 19), Judah's King Hezekiah prayed to the 'God of Israel' and the result was a resounding defeat for their enemies. The emphasis of his prayer was that his Lord would demonstrate that *he alone* was God (see 2 Kings 19.14-19).

Similar threats are heard today from those opposed to Israel. The former Grand Mufti of Jerusalem, Sheikh Ekrima Sabri, was denied the chance "to promote dialogue and a better understanding of the Palestinian narrative" in the UK Parliament[4] thanks, it seems, to an 18,000-strong petition. But the barefaced nerve of a man who has called for the destruction of Britain to attempt to infiltrate its parliament with his poisonous lies takes some beating.

This man represents the same ideological ethos as Islamic State. We are investing so much in the prevention of terror, yet are pathetically slow to recognise such threats to our democracy. 'We all worship the same God,' I hear so many naïve people (and politicians) say – even in church pews. But Sheikh Sabri says that when he enters the Al-Aqsa Mosque (on Jerusalem's Temple Mount) he is "filled with rage toward the Jews".[5]

Contrast this with Jesus' command to love our enemies and pray for our persecutors (see Matthew 5.44). As the Sheikh makes clear, Islam is committed to the destruction of 'infidels'. "The Muslim loves death and martyrdom," he says.

Part of the 'Palestinian narrative' is that Israel is guilty of human rights violations and of being an apartheid state. But the absurdity of these accusations is underlined by the emergence of a transgender Arab Christian from Nazareth as a new and public testimony against BDS, the boycott Israel campaign. Talleen Abu Hana, winner of the first Miss Trans Israel pageant, was guest of honour at the Israeli Embassy in Washington during LGBT Pride month.[6] Abu declared: "I'm happy to be Israeli because being Israeli means being truly free." And when an American journalist questioned Israel's record on human rights, she replied: "Are you crazy? In what other country in the Middle East can I live my life openly?"

Most Christians, including myself, do not agree with her lifestyle choice, but far more distasteful is the rank hypocrisy behind much liberal thought which sets politically-correct agendas that are inevitably contradictory.

In any case, Israel's restoration – according to biblical prophecy – is not yet complete. A restoration to the land (i.e. a political rebirth) is what we are witnessing today; this will be followed by a restoration to their Lord and Messiah, which is in the process of happening but still in the early stages.

One line of theological thought sees the fig tree (see Matthew 24.32) as a symbol of political Israel while the olive tree is seen as representing a return to its original purpose as a nation under God. The fig tree is certainly blossoming[7]as Israel becomes a powerful nation once more, but many of its inhabitants are still in rebellion against the Almighty.

Christians are privileged to have been grafted onto the natural olive tree of Israel (see Romans 11.11-24). But the day is coming when all Israel will finally turn to their Messiah (see Romans 11.26). All the hordes of hell are trying to stop that happening – hence the current battle – because it will usher in the Lord of glory who will crush the enemies of Israel and rule over the earth from Jerusalem for a thousand years of peace.

[1] Amir Tsarfati, *Behold Israel update*, YouTube, September 7 2017.
[2] *United with Israel*, September 7 2017.
[3] Michael Drosnin, *The Bible Code*, published by Orion in 1997, p91.
[4] *Christians United for Israel*, September 1 & 5 2017.
[5] Ibid., Sept 1.
[6] *Israel Today*, Aug/Sept 2017
[7] I appreciate that fig trees do not actually flower; blossoming is used here in the sense of flourishing and in leaf.

CHAPTER 17 – GERMANY'S 9/11

The dreadful consequences of touching the apple of God's eye

As we regularly recall with horror the terrorist atrocity witnessed by the whole world when New York's Twin Towers were reduced to rubble on September 11th 2001, few will be aware of an earlier 9/11 that destroyed an entire city.

It happened on the night of September 11th 1944, when the German city of Darmstadt suffered a devastating air raid by RAF pilots sent out from my hometown of Doncaster, headquarters of Bomber Command.

Twelve thousand residents were killed and many more made homeless amid ongoing controversy even in Britain as to whether it was really necessary as the war was almost won by then.

But as fire swept through the smouldering ruins, a devoted young German Christian wept bitterly over her nation's terrible sin against the Jewish people – she clearly saw the bombing as the judgment of God.

Basilea Schlink determined to do something about it and subsequently founded the *Evangelical Sisterhood of Mary*, dedicated to confessing the sin of her nation and making restitution with God's chosen people, chiefly by loving and serving them in whatever way they could.

More than 70 years later, the order is represented in nations across the globe, including Australia and the United States, and I have made several visits to their UK base near London where a coffee table book on their history recalls that fateful night in Darmstadt:

"For years our mothers had prayed for revival in the girls' Bible study groups they led; now their prayers were answered – far differently than they had ever expected. That night the girls encountered God in his holiness as Judge and Lord over life and death...

"Following that night of terror, there was a move among those young girls to bring sin into the light and receive forgiveness... God's moment had come. Out of the ashes emerged new life." [1]

Not surprisingly, the British-based sisters are deeply grieved at the rise of anti-Semitism all over Europe so soon after this terrible disaster caused by the Nazis' sickening murder of six million Jews in the death camps of Poland and Germany.

Have we still not learned that there are shocking consequences for those who touch the apple of God's eye, which is how the Bible refers to Israel (see Zechariah 2.8)?

Much of the talk among British Jews of late has been focused on which country to flee to if Jeremy Corbyn became Prime Minister as he has failed miserably to deal with the rise of anti-Semitism in his party, which has traditionally had the support of the Jewish community. According to my sources, many have already fled traditionally Jewish suburbs like Golders Green in north London in order to set up home in safer areas following a series of anti-Semitic incidents.

For Jews considering emigration, Israel is not necessarily their first choice of destination, I understand, because some see it as a move from the frying pan into the fire. But I disagree with that. I go along with a participant on BBC2's *We Are British Jews* programme,[2] who said that "It's the safest place in the world to be".

Yes, the Jewish state is surrounded by implacable enemies with an insatiable desire to wipe them off the map and, yes, they are threatened once more with annihilation. But Israel's security is very tight – and effective.

In any case, should physical safety be their only consideration? Isn't the safest place of all in the loving arms of God – the God of Israel? And his purpose is that they should return to the land of their forefathers, the land promised to Abraham as a permanent possession (see Gen 17.8). After all, the Tanakh prophets foretold of a great ingathering of Jews from every corner of the globe.

Almost half of world Jewry are now living in Israel and, according to the Bible, it would appear to be God's will that they should all return (Ezekiel 39.28). But don't misunderstand me. I do not wish to encourage persecution so that they feel forced to flee. Jewish contribution to European societies has been priceless – without the ongoing input of their high achievers we would all suffer. But woe to those whose intimidation does cause them to leave; for they will come under a curse (Genesis 12.3).

Nevertheless, it is God's purpose that his chosen people should be back in the land before Messiah returns. Yes, there will be a battle over Jerusalem, and the nations will come against it, but the Lord will intervene and defeat the enemies of Israel, once and for all. (See Zechariah 12-14.)

When Jesus ascended to heaven as his perplexed disciples watched in wonder, angels explained to them that he would one day return in the same way he had left – and this took place on the Mount of Olives, east of Jerusalem (see Acts 1.11).

The prophet Zechariah confirms this – that Christ would indeed place his feet on the Mt of Olives and that the Jewish nation would have their eyes opened as they recognise Jesus as the One they had pierced (see Zech 12.10).

The Messiah for whom Jews have longed will appear on earth, and they will acknowledge that he has been here before – as the suffering servant (see Isaiah 53). Although they will mourn over what they did to him (we all need to confess our sin in order to be cleansed), their hearts will be sprinkled clean – and *all Israel will be saved* (see Ezekiel 36.25, Zech 13.1, Romans 11.26).

Jesus is coming again – and the establishing of the people of Israel in their land is a major sign.

[1] *A Celebration of God's Unfailing Love*, published by the Evangelical Sisters of Mary.
[2] A two-part series screened in September 2018.

An unholy alliance

Just as news was coming through of failed talks between Jewish leaders and Britain's (then) Labour Party chief Jeremy Corbyn, who had been embroiled in an ongoing scandal over anti-Semitism since his taking on the leadership, I was watching a TV presenter telling the harrowing story of anti-Semitic butchery in the land of the reporter's great-grandparents.

Following yet another debate on the subject in Parliament, during which Jewish Labour MPs received standing ovations after giving testimony to the flak they had to endure, Mr Corbyn met with representatives of the Board of Deputies of British Jews and the Jewish Leadership Council.

But they were not happy with the result. In a joint statement, they said he had refused to agree to any of their demands, which included banning MPs from appearing with members under investigation by the party on the issue.

Mr Corbyn consistently acted and spoke as though he was the innocent party in all this, committing himself to strong statements of support for the Jewish community, but without being able to back it up with action.

That is surely because his hard-left agenda had attracted a swathe of followers who were, by definition, natural allies of those who hate Israel which, ironically, also includes far-right extremists and terror groups committed to the Jewish state's destruction. An unholy alliance, if ever there was one!

Television presenter Simon Schama, meanwhile, used some grisly historical facts to illustrate the depravity of anti-Semites who, in the Russian pogrom of 1905, mercilessly decapitated Jewish people and tore their children apart limb from limb.

In the penultimate episode of *The Story of the Jews* on the BBC4 channel, he traced the history of his people in that part of the world; how they were forced to live in rural communities so that they were unable to compete with Gentile city businessmen. But they made the most of life and worked for the benefit of each other while always living in fear of assault – just for being Jewish.

Fortunately, many were able to escape to America which, with Zion not yet an option, became their New World paradise. Some two-and-a-half million Jews from Eastern Europe sailed to New York from the 1880s to 1920s and, in a substantial way, helped to build modern America – even shaping the emerging film industry in Hollywood and writing 'the Great American Songbook'. In the latter case, the lyrics often reflected their own longing for peace and safety. In the hit Broadway musical *West Side Story*, Leonard Bernstein (the son of Jewish immigrants from Russia) and fellow Jew Stephen Sondheim would compose: "There's a place for us, somewhere a place for us, peace and quiet and open air, wait for us somewhere..."

Over the Rainbow (from *The Wizard of Oz*) reflected the same sentiment: "Somewhere, over the rainbow, way up high; there's a land that I've heard of, once in a lullabye... Somewhere, over the rainbow, skies are blue, and the dreams that you dare to dream really do come true."

Yet just as Yip Harburg collected his Oscar for the song in 1940, the Nazi reign of terror was about to be unleashed in Europe with demonic fury. If we claim to be a civilised society, then mere words from Mr Corbyn are not enough. Action is required. I'm sure he does not want to find himself backing the wrong side in a Middle East conflict that might erupt at any moment.

For just as Jerusalem reverberated to the sound of singing and dancing in celebration of 70 years as a nation, threats to Israel's existence were as belligerent as ever. They are surrounded by vicious enemies – specifically Hezbollah to the north and Hamas to the south – with sponsors Iran vowing to wipe them out.

More worryingly, the Ayatollahs are infuriated by Israeli attacks on military targets in Syria designed to deter any further incursion of Iranian influence in the region. Adding to the toxic mix is the involvement of Russia. So it could all blow up in our faces. Therefore, cool heads are called for – but not appeasers backing down at every threat of a dictator. That is why President Trump is such a breath of fresh air, insisting that the nuclear deal agreed by his predecessor must not be extended as it will only further encourage Iran to commit genocide against Israel.

He has also torn up the 'rule book' of Middle East diplomacy by ceasing to refer to Judea, Samaria and the Golan Heights as 'occupied' territories, infuriating the Palestinians in the process. As with the reality of recognising Jerusalem as Israel's capital, the President is simply going a step further by bringing down the curtain on the fantasy world of Palestinian claims to the land.

They flatly refused the offer (of these territories) as part of the UN's Partition Plan in 1947, Jordan then illegally annexed it during the 1948 War of Independence, and Israel took it back in 1967.

In fact, there was a time not long ago when Arabs refused to be known as Palestinians. When 30,000 Jews, along with a few hundred Arabs, volunteered to serve with the British forces during World War II, they were permitted to wear a 'Palestine' shoulder patch. But the Arabs would not wear it: "We are not Palestinians; we are Arabs," they responded.[1]

Anyway, the mountains of Judea and Samaria represent the heartland of Israel. Far from inflaming the situation, President Trump's recognition of this disputed territory as belonging to Israel paves the way for practical thinking in the real world. Here is a President who will not buckle under pressure, but does want to see real peace. No amount of compromise over these past 70 years has ultimately done the trick. Let us continue to pray for the peace of Jerusalem.

[1] *Whose Land?* by Dov Chaikin, *Israel Today*, January 2018.

CHAPTER 18 – BRITAIN'S ROLE

That Britain has played a key role in Israel's restoration is in no doubt, but the tragedy is that she also betrayed the Jews in their darkest hour.

Jeremy Hunt's apology, when Foreign Secretary, over Britain's treatment of Jews during the Mandate of Palestine is an encouraging development to be greatly applauded. But it has been a long time in coming. Not from him, I mean, but from successive British governments. He is believed to be the first holder of this office to have acknowledged our criminal behaviour over the plight of Jewish refugees trying to escape the Nazis.

Calling it a 'black moment' in history, it involved denying entrance to the very homeland we had pledged to help recreate for the Jews at the time they needed it most. And Britain has been under a curse ever since, fulfilling the negative part of Genesis 12.3 – that those who curse the seed of Abraham would face judgment.

Mr Hunt was addressing the annual parliamentary reception of Conservative Friends of Israel, hailing the "very strong relationship" between Britain and Israel and declaring Israel's right to self-defence as being "absolutely unconditional". But he added: "There have been some black moments when we have done the wrong thing such as the 1939 White Paper which capped the number of visas issued to Jews wanting to go to the British mandate of Palestine."[1]

Anne Heelis, who heads up a group[2] dedicated to comforting those who suffered as a result of British Mandate policies, said this "wonderful development" had come just a day after confession for our role was made during a Holocaust memorial service in Northern Ireland.

"Hundreds of thousands of Jewish people could have escaped death in the Nazi concentration camps if they had been allowed free entry into their ancient homeland, but Britain cruelly blocked this way of escape by severely restricting Jewish immigration," Anne said.

Those who had been praying for a change of heart were "deeply grateful" for this development, she added, and though Mr Hunt's remarks were "most welcome", they did not amount to an apology.

"They are indeed a wonderful answer to prayer and a great encouragement to continue praying with broken hearts for our Government to make a full apology to Israel. There is still a deep wound in the heart of many Israelis as a result of Britain's misconduct of the Mandate."

Rosie Ross, whose organisation Repairing the Breach has also been working with those who suffered under the Mandate, said Mr Hunt's statement was "a major breakthrough" that was clearly an answer to prayer, some of which has been specifically targeted at the Foreign Office. And she also looks forward to a full apology.

Because the 1917 Balfour Declaration – promising to do all we could to aid Jewish repatriation – had subsequently been legitimised both by the 1920 Treaty of San Remo and the League of Nations in 1922, Britain had all the delegated power she needed to rescue many thousands of God's chosen people from disaster.

But they failed to act because of Arab opposition, choosing to pursue a policy of appeasement that had never worked with Hitler. And we are still suffering the consequences, with the Middle East up in flames, the rest of Europe in turmoil and Britain in particular in a state of utter chaos and bewilderment.

We lost our empire, beginning with India in 1947, along with much of our power and influence and, as we succumbed increasingly to secularisation, we broke loose from our moral moorings. We also lost our sovereignty as we got sucked into the godless European whirlpool which further weakened our Judaeo-Christian foundations.

All this leaves us frantically splashing about in an ocean of confusion while much of the political elite have been engaged in a desperate bid to avoid carrying out the people's wish of regaining our national pride.

It is worth noting that the three longest-serving British Prime Ministers of the modern era – Harold Wilson, Margaret Thatcher and Tony Blair – were unflinching in their support for the Jews. I will say more about Wilson shortly. Mrs Thatcher, for her part, not only helped save a Jewish girl's life from the Holocaust but also faithfully served her strongly Jewish constituency throughout her parliamentary career and Mr Blair inaugurated the annual Holocaust Memorial Day to help ensure it does not happen again.

Others, including Neville Chamberlain, Anthony Eden, James Callaghan and even Winston Churchill, disappeared from the political scene after letting God's ancient people down.[3]

Where are the great empires of the past – Egyptian, Assyrian, Babylonian, Greek and Roman – who have treated the *apple of God's eye* (see Zech 2.8) with disdain? They are buried in the dust of history.

With this in mind, Christians United for Israel UK launched *Operation Mordecai* to highlight the threat to Israel and the West posed by Iran, with the primary aim of ensuring that Britain positions itself on the right side of history by defending Israel against tyranny.

The campaign takes its inspiration from the biblical account of Esther's cousin Mordecai who, having heard of a plot to annihilate the Jews, sought the Lord, warned about what was planned and took action.

Let us not go the way of Amnesty International, calling for a boycott of Israel's tourism industry in Judea and Samaria, accusing the Jewish state of "occupation, human rights violations and war crimes".[4]

Paul Charney, chairman of the Zionist Federation of the UK and Ireland, said the humanitarian organisation thus demonstrates its lack of neutrality by whitewashing any Palestinian culpability for the conflict.

"Amnesty must recognise the incitement, the children's television programmes encouraging violence and terrorism, and the salaries to convicted terrorists under the Palestinian Authority's 'Pay to Slay' policy, to name but a few of the many disgraces which bear much responsibility for the current situation."

He added that such boycotts harm the very people they wish to help.

Meanwhile Labour ties with its sister party in Israel have been officially cut over its handling of anti-Semitism, which bodes ill for any potential Labour-led government. It was in 2016 that Mr Corbyn refused an invitation from Isaac Herzog, then leader of Israel's Labour Party, to visit Israel and tour the Yad Vashem Holocaust museum. Herzog, now chairman of the Jewish Agency for Israel, is reported to be "extremely distraught" by what is happening in Britain's Labour Party.[5]

So should we be. And our Foreign Office has a bad record of dealings with Israel; so let us hope Mr Hunt's statement signals a turning of the tide.

For we do not wish to be numbered among Israel's enemies, of whom the Psalmist wrote: *Come, they say, let us destroy them as a nation, that the name of Israel be remembered no more* (Psalm 83.4).

And Psalm 146 adds: *Do not put your trust in princes, in mortal men, who cannot save. When their spirit departs, they return to the ground; on that very day their plans come to nothing* (verses 3-4).

[1] *United with Israel*, February 1st 2019.

[2] *Nachamu Ami* (Comfort ye my people – Isaiah 40.1).

[3] *Defending Christian Zionism*, David Pawson (Anchor) pp. 80 and 116.

[4] *United with Israel*, 30th January 2019.

[5] *Jerusalem News Network*, 30th January 2019, quoting *Jerusalem Post*.

Footballers Salute the Fuehrer!

Bearing in mind the obvious success of President Trump's "Don't mess with me" strategy in getting dictators to the negotiating table, surely lessons can be learnt from this. It certainly gives a whole new meaning to 'playing the trump card'. But the stubborn Europeans refuse to take note, or even learn from history. Did not Jesus indicate that wisdom – and recognition of his Lordship in particular – was hidden from "the wise", but revealed to "little children"? (see Matthew 11.25).

I am more staggered than ever at the lengths to which the British Government has gone to appease dictators since learning for the first time that the England football team had, in 1938, raised a Nazi salute to Hitler in front of a crowd of 105,000 before a friendly match against Germany in Berlin – on the orders of the Foreign Office![1]

This was apparently designed to pave the way for Neville Chamberlain's efforts to appease the Fuehrer, instead of squaring up to him as Churchill was later to do. (A copy of the infamous 'Nazi salute' photo, reproduced in the *Daily Mail*, was sent to Britain's then Foreign Secretary Boris Johnson from his Russian counterpart Sergey Lavrov in response to Johnson's suggestion that Russia was using the World Cup for propaganda purposes in the same way that Hitler had done with the 1936 Olympics.)

This shameful (1938) episode in Britain's history was a natural progression of their foreign policy in bending over backwards to keep the Arabs happy throughout the 1920s and 1930s when they were supposed to be preparing a home for the Jewish people. Buckling under the pressure of Muslim-inspired riots over the prospect of a Jewish nation in their midst, Britain betrayed both their international obligation and their own Balfour Declaration promising to do all they could to ensure that Zionist aspirations were met.

The Israeli-Palestinian conflict could well have been nipped in the bud if we had acted with more integrity and courage. And after all these years, Britain is still batting for the wrong side by refusing to follow President Trump's lead in recognising Jerusalem as the Jewish capital. Fear of Muslim-Arab fury, rather than pleasing God in blessing Israel, once again turns us into cowards presiding over the potential ruin of our country (see Isaiah 60.12).

Former Prime Minister Theresa May and her European allies also refused to take President Trump (and Israeli PM Benjamin Netanyahu) seriously over the danger posed by Iran, insisting on sticking to the Obama-led nuclear deal designed to keep the lid on the rogue state's weapons build-up. The Ayatollah's threat of removing and eradicating the "malignant cancerous tumour" he calls Israel[2] is shrugged off in a manner reminiscent of the 1930s, when Hitler's rantings were not taken seriously.

Mr Netanyahu says it is "amazing that at the beginning of the 21st century, somebody talks about destroying Israel – that means destroying another six million-plus Jews...."[3]

This is the same country that was behind the bombing of the Buenos Aires Jewish community centre in 1994, leaving 85 dead, an atrocity that has blighted Argentina ever since. Our weakness with Iran seems to chime with our long-held stance on its terrorist proxy Hezbollah who had been free to parade their hate-filled views on Israel through the streets of London despite ongoing calls for an outright ban which has thankfully now at last been imposed.

Refusing for some time to apply a full ban on the organisation (in recognising separate political and military wings which Hezbollah itself does not acknowledge) not only encouraged 'hate speech' which is supposed to be illegal, but is also obviously against the interests of our 300,000-strong Jewish community as well as Israel.

By sanctioning the belligerence of those who seek Israel's demise, we were certainly not being a blessing to the seed of Abraham, and were thus in further danger of bringing a curse upon our nation (Genesis 12.3).

Can we not learn from Brazil where two million Christians took to the streets of Sao Paulo for their annual *March for Jesus*? According to one report, the crowd were waving Israeli flags while cheering and praying for the Jewish state.[4] For the first time in nearly 20 years of the event, Jewish officials were invited to attend. Addressing the gathering, Israel's consul Dori Goren said: "Attending the march is our way to express our gratitude for the evangelical people and the Brazilian people."

Argentinian evangelist Andrew Palau, son of Luis, preached the gospel and a "sea of hands" were raised in response to his call to faith and repentance. Tens of thousands of Iranians have also expressed support for Israel in a Twitter campaign to distance themselves from the opinions of their regime.[5]

Christians who know their Bible and are committed to following Jesus are also serious about their love for Jews. For it was they who gave us the patriarchs, the prophets, the Bible itself and indeed the Lord Jesus.

Since God consistently proclaims his unfailing love for his chosen people despite their repeated backsliding, Bible believers naturally follow the same path so that it becomes the case that if you love Jesus, you find yourself also loving the Jew. I recently heard of a Gazan Arab brought up to hate the Jews who has started to love them after meeting Jesus. But now his life is in danger.

Christians are those who follow Jesus – "despised and

rejected of men" (Isaiah 53.3) – and are thus prepared to suffer abuse and ridicule as he did. In the same way they will also be ready to wave Israeli flags, which is to swim very much against the tide in almost every generation. True Christians are happy to nail their colours to the mast – and to support the real victims of society, not necessarily those groups beloved of our 'woke'(politically-correct) world.

So why do British Christians (on the whole) not get the connection between following Jesus and befriending the Jews? Could it perhaps be something to do with Pentecost? For Jesus explained that the Holy Spirit, poured out at Pentecost, would *guide you into all the truth* (see John 16.13). And he also said: *Whoever is ashamed of me and my words, the Son of Man will be ashamed of him when he comes in his glory and in the glory of the Father and of the holy angels* (Luke 9.26).

[1] *Daily Mail*, 9th June 2018.

[2] *Jerusalem News Service*, quoting *Medialine/Jerusalem Post*, 6th June 2018 – Ayatollah Ali Khamenei, Iran's supreme leader, later sought to clarify his position by saying that the conflict should be resolved through a referendum among "all real Palestinians including Muslims, Jews and Christians" who trace their roots back to before the creation of Israel in 1948. *World Israel News & Associated Press*, 11th June 2018.

[3] An obvious reference to the Holocaust and the fact that more than six million Jews now live in Israel – Ibid.

[4] *Gateway News*, South Africa, 7th June 2018:
http://gatewaynews.co.za/

[5] *Jewish News Syndicate*, 13th June 2018.

The Forgotten Friend of Israel

In attempting recently to address the important issue of roots – both of Christianity and of Western civilisation as a whole – I was somewhat diverted along a different *route*. In looking up a verse from Isaiah, where he refers to the *root of Jesse* (one of many prophecies of the coming Messiah, Jesus), I was reminded[1] of the fact that former British Prime Minister Harold Wilson had made much of a text from this passage in support of his Zionist views, spelt out in his book *The Chariot of Israel*[2] and clearly inspired by his strong Christian faith. (I am reliably informed that both Harold and his wife Mary were Bible-believing Congregationalists, to which he also owed his brand of Christian socialism).

The text in question, Isaiah 11.11, refers to a second return of Jewish exiles,[3] which trumps the notion that such prophecies were all fulfilled with the return from Babylon.

I believe this is very significant in light of the ongoing controversy over rising anti-Semitism within the Labour Party, of which Wilson was a long-time leader and the only occupant of No 10 Downing Street to have won four general elections. By tragic contrast, Labour leader Jeremy Corbyn openly embraced those who wished to destroy Israel.

Writing for the *Jewish Chronicle* on the 50th anniversary of Wilson's first election victory,[4] Robert Philpot dubbed him "the forgotten friend of Israel" who sprang to her aid in 1967 and 1973 and whose first overseas visit after leaving office in 1976 was to Israel, where he received an honorary doctorate and inspected a forest near Nazareth that had been named after him!

In Parliament he described the Jewish state "by any test... the only democracy in [the] region" and his book was described by his Home Secretary and Chancellor of the Exchequer Roy Jenkins as "one of the most strongly Zionist tracts ever written by a non-Jew".

Tragically, however, his devotion to the cause of Israel contrasts sharply with today's Labour left from whose ranks he originally hailed.[5]

Which takes me back to my starting point, for the survival of our Judaeo-Christian civilisation will depend entirely on whether we remain connected to our biblical roots. If we cut ourselves off from our godly heritage, the 'sap' that gives us life, direction and purpose will no longer flow, with the result that our culture will wither and die like a tree pulled from the ground.

In late January/early February (in the northern hemisphere) we begin to witness the shoots that produce flowers like snowdrops, crocuses and daffodils pointing the way to another springtime. These beauties come from roots (or bulbs) buried in the ground for many months.

Christianity was the new spring in the purposes of God that emerged from the roots of Judaism. According to St Paul's letter to the Roman Christians, who had to be reminded that God was not finished with his chosen people, Gentile believers *now share in the nourishing sap from the olive root* (of Israel) ... *You do not support the root, but the root supports you,* he thundered (see Rom 11.17f).

This should encourage us to put our trust squarely in the God of Israel, and his Son, the Jewish Messiah, Jesus, *the Lion of the tribe of Judah, the root of David* (see Revelation 5.5) and Isaiah's *root of Jesse* (David's father, see Isa 11.10) who will draw the nations (Gentiles) to himself.

In this respect it is also significant that, as discussed earlier, there is a strain of Gentile 'blood'[6] in Jesus, through his ancestor Ruth, the Moabitess, King David's great-grandmother, a wonderful woman of virtue who threw in her lot with her Jewish mother-in-law Naomi.

Still on this theme, Isaiah's discussion of roots is related to a springtime for the nation of Israel that surely speaks of today with its reference to a second return from exile, this time not just from Babylon but *from the four quarters of the earth* (Isa 11.11f) including *the islands of the sea* considered by some theologians to refer to the British Isles.

This passage also speaks of a coming millennial age of perfect peace when *the wolf will live with the lamb, the leopard will lie down with the goat, the calf and the lion and the yearling together...* (see Isa 11.6).

They will neither harm nor destroy on all my holy mountain, for the earth will be full of the knowledge of the Lord as the waters cover the sea (Isa 11.9).

As for Israel, the Lord speaks emphatically of final restoration through the prophet Amos, concluding with the words: *I will plant Israel in their own land, never again to be uprooted...* (Amos 9.15).

---

[1] See *Defending Christian Zionism* by David Pawson (Anchor, see pp.80 and 116).

[2] Ibid.

[3] The text begins: *In that day the Lord will reach out his hand a second time to reclaim the remnant that is left of his people....*

[4] Wilson, true friend of Israel – The Jewish Chronicle, 27th October 2014, https://www.thejc.com/comment/comment/wilson-true-friend-of-israel-1.58771

[5] It is only fair to record that after chairing the debate in Parliament to mark Holocaust Memorial Day (January 27), my own MP, Dame Rosie Winterton (Labour, Doncaster Central), said: "It is shocking that many British Jews are considering leaving this country.... We must support those in our community who feel threatened. This means tackling and condemning anti-Semitism wherever we find it, including in the Labour Party."

[6] Obviously not actual blood, as Jesus was born of the Holy Spirit through the Virgin Mary, though certainly ancestral as Jewish genealogy would confirm.

British Betrayal Revisited

Evidence of further shameful acts of anti-Semitism carried out by British officials during its charge over the territory formerly known as Palestine has come to light of late.[1]

A special 70th anniversary ceremony was held near Haifa at which UK representatives shared a 'declaration of sorrow' for the way our country treated Jews in the years leading up to the rebirth of their nation in 1948. Some shocking facts were shared by Holocaust survivors and others attending the ceremony, organised by *Love Never Fails*, an alliance of Christian groups supporting the Jewish state.

The event took place at Atlit, a former detention camp where Jewish refugees were held as part of British policy to limit immigration to the region, adding further trauma to a people who had already suffered terribly under the Nazis. Granted a League of Nations mandate to prepare a safe homeland for Jews, Britain instead interred them behind barbed wire complete with watchtowers.

Among those who shared their harrowing stories of the time were Hannah Avrutsky. A survivor of the notorious Warsaw ghetto,[2] she was hidden in a monastery before being smuggled to the *Exodus* ship bound for Israel in 1947, only to face a British naval blockade and be sent back to a Displaced Persons' camp in Germany, where so many of her people had been murdered!

Ben Zion Drutin spoke of being hospitalised after being wounded by the British on board the *Exodus* and then held in Atlit for six months. Arie Itamar, who was eight years old on the *Exodus*, compared Israel to a "betrayed lover" during the Mandate. Pinchas Kahane spoke of his parents' escape from Auschwitz, his birth in a Cyprus detention camp and how Britain prevented them leaving the camps until February 1949, well after the establishment of the State of Israel.

Dr Miri Nehari, whose father had been a leader in mobilising the escape of Jews from Europe after the Holocaust, read out a British telegram to the Polish government-in-exile asking them to close the borders to escaping Jews.

Zehavit Blumenfeld, whose 70th birthday has coincided with that of Israel's, said: "I do not forget, but I forgive." She was born in the Cyprus detention camps where 53,000 Jewish refugees from the Holocaust were interned by the British. She and others were moved by the warmth and sympathy of the Christians who came to express their sorrow, and hoped that Prince William's visit (later that year) would be an important step towards reconciliation.

The testimonies concluded with stories of British collusion with Arab terror during the Mandate. Noam Arnon, representing the Hebron Jewish Community, spoke on behalf of those who had survived the 1929 massacre there, outlining British complicity.

Zehava Fuchs witnessed the Hadassah convoy massacre as a girl in 1948 when the British had deliberately not intervened to rescue Jewish passengers – 78 people, mainly doctors and nurses, were killed in the attack by Arab terrorists. Zehava is still unable to attend a barbeque as it reminds her of the smell of burning flesh.

Rachel Rust, daughter of a former British officer who served in Palestine, confessed her deep sorrow at the cruel treatment handed out by the British army. On a positive note, Rita Offenbach shared how her mother was among 180 Jewish fighters rescued after being besieged by Arabs attacking their convoy. Another paid tribute to British officer Orde Wingate who is still much loved in Israel for having laid the foundations of the Israeli Defence Force in creating special night squads.

The declaration of sorrow read, in part: "We grieve that (Britain's policies) led to the deaths of hundreds of thousands of Jews who could have escaped Hitler's 'final solution' if the gates to their ancient homeland had been fully open."

Film-maker Hugh Kitson[3] expressed sorrow not only for the failures of the Mandate, but also for the fact that today's British Government fails to recognise Israeli sovereignty over their own capital city. Many Israelis are still waiting to hear an apology from Britain for her betrayal of Israel in breaking a pledge to prepare a safe refuge for the Jewish people. Israel came into being without our help in the end, but not before many lives were unnecessarily lost due to the delay. There is still a need for much repentance and reconciliation.

---

[1] My thanks to Rosie Ross, Israel's *Love Never Fails* representative, for the Atlit report, and to her colleague Anne Heelis for passing it on to me.
[2] Where Jews were herded into a cramped, unsanitary location as a staging post for being transported to death camps.
[3] Hugh Kitson's latest documentary *Whose Land?* explores Israel's historic and legal rights to their land.

British royalty returns from 'exile'

Meanwhile Prince William in 2018 made a first-ever official visit to Israel by a British Royal during which he paid his respects at the tomb of his great-grandmother, Princess Alice of Greece, recognised by Jerusalem's Yad Vashem Holocaust Museum as 'righteous among the nations' for hiding a Jewish family from the Nazis during the war.

Although Queen Elizabeth has travelled the world more than most, she has never set foot in Israel, the land which gave birth to the Christian faith she so devoutly follows. The long exile from the modern Jewish state by British royalty is perhaps complex, but seems to reflect Foreign Office policy, which generally amounts to appeasement of the surrounding Arab nations. Nevertheless, we trust and pray that the Duke of Cambridge will have helped bring peace to the region where he walked in the footsteps of Jesus, the Prince of Peace.

The responsibility for Britain's fortune or failure will inevitably have much to do with how we treat Israel. We stand at the crossroads with a great opportunity to bless the Jews – to work with them towards a peaceful future in the Middle East or to work against them in appeasement of their enemies as we have done for much of the last century. Which road will we take? Will we step out in faith – honouring the God of Israel – or succumb to fear of the repercussions?

CHAPTER 19 – THE VIEW FROM ISRAEL

Now I want to tell you the story of how a hot seaside property unlocked the door to the nations. Having lived in a 'bubble' during a lengthy tour of Israel in the autumn of 2017, visiting sites connected with the gospel that has changed the world, it came as a shock to re-enter the atmosphere of nations in turmoil – Germany in trouble, Mugabe finally deposed in Zimbabwe and Britain continuing to fight both internal and external battles over Brexit.

There is perhaps a message in this strange transition – the countries in difficulty have been built largely on a Judeo-Christian ethos, but have been rapidly casting off its 'shackles' in favour of a no-holds-barred secular humanist system.

The last eleven days of our four-week trip was spent at Jaffa, at the southern end of Tel Aviv, an old port city known in Bible times as Joppa, where the Apostle Peter had a vision that brought the good news of Jesus to the entire Gentile world. He was staying at Simon the Tanner's house (which is still there) and was resting on the rooftop when he fell into a trance and saw a vision of all kinds of animals including those regarded by Jews as unclean.

This was not, as some suppose, a licence to eat pork, but a supernatural message that he was not to regard Gentiles as being unable to be reached by the gospel. It coincided with a similar encounter experienced by a Roman centurion called Cornelius in the coastal city of Caesarea, some 40 miles north. Cornelius was a god-fearing man who loved the Jews, and an angel appeared to him saying that his prayers had been heard and he was to send for a man called Peter, who was staying with Simon the Tanner at his house by the sea. The rest is history.

Cornelius and his extended family heard the triumphant message of the gospel and were filled with the Holy Spirit, just as the Jewish disciples had been on the day of Pentecost. This opened the door for the good news to spread across the nations, bringing kindness, compassion and justice with it which helped to establish a powerful force known as Western civilisation.

Tragically, the Jewish people were exiled throughout the world within a generation of Jesus' death and resurrection after the Romans destroyed Jerusalem and massacred many of its inhabitants. But Christians eventually translated the Bible into hundreds of languages, further enabling the gospel to spread.

Yet God had not forgotten the people with whom he had made an unbreakable covenant and, in fulfilment of many ancient prophecies, the scattered seed of Abraham finally took root in the Promised Land after an absence of nearly two thousand years.

Just as the gospel was originally 'exported' from Joppa, so it has now become a re-entry point for Jews[1] – not only coming back to the land, but in being restored to their Lord. My stay there was unplanned as I was initially prevented from returning to the UK due to new restrictions on 'foreigners' like me. Though South African-born and still a citizen of that country by choice (my wife is British), I have lived in England for nearly fifty years. Yet I now apparently need a visa – though an inked stamp in an old passport sent over by neighbours eventually proved sufficient!

We stayed in a guesthouse which also hosted two Messianic congregations as well as a music school led by a former director of the Russian Philharmonic Orchestra. It was a very moving experience to witness hands and eyes lifted to the skies in adoration of the Lord in a revived form of ancient Hebrew as we worshipped together on a Friday night – the start of the Jewish Sabbath. Headsets were provided for Russian members and English visitors like us.

Committed to the spiritual restoration of Israel, this peaceful oasis is perfectly placed to go some way towards achieving this divine goal, with its great potential for reaching out to Greater Tel Aviv where almost half the country's Jewish population lives. The whole ethos of the place beats loudly with a heart of love for the largely lost world around them, who find welcome, warmth and hospitality in this gem of an international community steeped in history and within a short walk of some of the most significant biblical sites, not to mention magnificent beaches.

Life in Tel Aviv is tough, rough and expensive! I watched poor people struggling as they waited in the swamp of a filthy launderette while others begged for food and wandered the streets with no apparent hope. But there are also swanky high-rise hotels and a bustling downtown area overshadowed by skyscrapers, with many indulging in a hedonistic lifestyle of clubs and coffee bars. But they are living in a bubble, afraid to confront reality.

I met one of them at the airport, a charming young lady commuting between London and Tel Aviv, confessing to being a 'secular Jew' yet listening with interest when I shared of our study tour learning about the Jewish roots of the Christian faith. She admitted to being shocked when she left her 'bubble' to visit friends in the north who lived within the sound of exploding bombs across the border in Syria where violence continues to rage.

But even in Tel Aviv the mangled wreck of a beachside cafe stands as a stark reminder of the constant threat facing its inhabitants – a bloody terror attack killed 21 mainly young people enjoying a night out there just three months before 9/11.

Although in general we sensed an atmosphere of profound peace throughout our tour, there were a couple of incidents to remind us of the conflict that has raged there ever since the Jews began returning to the land. The IDF bombing of a Hamas terror tunnel raised a security alert as the group had promised vengeance, and a suicide bombing in a Druze village just across the border in Syria caused another alarm – and a long wait at a checkpoint.

The resettling of Jews in Israel following their long exile is very reminiscent of the time of Nehemiah 2,500 years ago when they returned from 70 years in Babylon. Nehemiah was given authority by King Artaxerxes of Persia to restore the broken walls of Jerusalem, but his work was strongly opposed by others in the surrounding lands. Now the Jews have returned once more to the Promised Land, and yet again they face fierce opposition.

Nehemiah's men built the walls using one hand for construction and the other to hold a weapon – exactly as Israel has developed since the birth of the modern state as ancient ruins have been rebuilt, barren wastes have been richly cultivated and wars have been won against all odds.

When, in Nehemiah's time, the city was finally rebuilt and made secure, Ezra was assigned to read the Book of the Law, as a result of which the people repented of how far they had strayed from God's rule. And now the Jewish people are returning to the Lord once more in fulfilment of ancient prophecies, with Jeremiah adding that there will come a day when they will all know the Lord, *from the least of them to the greatest* (see Jer 31.34).

If Jews are thus turning back to God, it means the return of Jesus is that much closer (see Zech 12.10 & 14.4, Romans

11.26). But what of the nations to whom the gospel was graciously given? Will they be among the sheep or the goats on Judgment Day? (See Matthew 25.31-46.) On the closing page of the Bible, Jesus says: *Yes, I am coming soon.*

Come, Lord Jesus!

[1] Tel Aviv's Ben Gurion Airport is not far away

Jews speak up for Christians

A relatively new phenomenon has emerged on the Middle East scene in the form of Jews standing up for persecuted Christians. It is a true wonder, bearing in mind the shocking history of Jewish persecution at the hands of the 'church' over the centuries. But it is also no doubt a warm response to the growing worldwide support for Israel among Christian people, especially in Africa.

And so, keen to build on this developing friendship, the Israeli government has begun hosting unprecedented media summits in Jerusalem for Christian journalists from around the world.

Prime Minister Benjamin Netanyahu used the first such occasion to speak up for embattled Christians in Iran and neighbouring Syria. "Christians today have been lashed for sipping wine during prayer services," he said, "brutally tortured for doing nothing more than practising their faith. Some world leaders are willing to ignore this oppression and seek to appease Iran, but I am not one of them."[1]

Yes, even much of the Western church has been silent on the issue, apparently indifferent to their suffering. Canon Andrew White, known as the 'Vicar of Baghdad' and also speaking in Jerusalem, asked why, adding: "Here we see Jews standing with us, but where is the Church?"[2]

White saw much of his large congregation murdered in the crisis that followed the invasion of Iraq, and thousands of Christians have been forced to flee Islamic State terror. Does this weak response to the plight of persecuted Christians reflect the flabbiness of our faith? Do we simply fail to comprehend what it must be like because we are so comfortable and thus unable to identify with what suffering for Christ means? For the most part, we are not even willing to stand up for what we believe in case we should be arrested for 'hate speech' or 'Islamophobia'.

While some have indeed spoken out, and paid dearly for it, the rest of us have been intimidated into silence as we retreat into our holy huddles. But if we cannot stand the moderate heat now, how will we fare when the temperature is turned up and we are called to endure the kind of persecution Jesus predicted for his followers?

Be on your guard, he warned. *You will be handed over to the local councils and flogged in the synagogues.... You will be hated by everyone because of me, but the one who stands firm to the end will be saved* (see Matthew 10.17, 22).

Many Christians remained silent while Jews were hauled off to the gas chambers and, although now somewhat more secure in their own state, they are still in grave danger, and we must not fail them this time. And yet they are prepared to help us!

It is time to forsake cowardice and match the sort of courage which Christians in some parts of the world are having to exhibit in bucket-loads. Take the believers in Iran, for example, to which Mr Netanyahu drew the media's attention. Despite the danger of following Jesus there, 20 Iranian Christians recently nailed their colours to the mast in a mass baptism. "I've been waiting for this moment for nearly nine years," said one convert. "This was my wish before I die," said another.

Christianity is growing there by leaps and bounds amid reports of Muslims encountering Jesus through dreams and visions. "We have been praying for years that Iranian people believe in Yeshua and get baptized. Now this dream is coming true," said a convert whose brother was murdered for his faith in 1994.[3]

Another highly dangerous place to be a Christian is North Korea, where believers are actually meeting in holes in the ground, just as the faith heroes of old had done according to Hebrews 11.38.[4]

A missionary friend of mine sometimes travels to a part of Africa that is equally dangerous, infested as it is by the Al Shabaab terror organisation. As a result, some Christians are forced to sleep in the forest! But my friend was determined to bring comfort to them with his inspiring teaching skills, so he made his way there despite Foreign Office warnings to avoid the region, and the fact he could not even be covered by travel insurance for that part of his journey. On top of that, he nearly died from an infection he picked up on his last visit to the area! That takes courage, but he said it was worth it just to see the smiling faces of his brothers so happy and encouraged to see him.

I conclude with the heartwarming story of Israeli tennis player Dudi Sela who, due to the courage of his religious convictions, turned down the chance of reaching the semi-finals of an ATP (Association of Tennis Professionals) Tour event. Just eight minutes into the deciding set, he realised it was almost sunset, which marked the beginning of Yom Kippur, the Day of Atonement (the holiest day of the year for Jews). So the 32-year-old informed the umpire of his decision to retire and left the court.[5]

The match was originally scheduled for Yom Kippur itself (i.e. the following day), but was changed to start before the fast following pressure from Israeli tennis officials. Unfortunately for Dudi (then ranked 77 in the world), his quarter-final clash went to three sets and could not be finished in time.

The Day of Atonement, when Jews seek forgiveness for sins committed over the past year, is ultimately fulfilled by the coming of Yeshua, their Messiah, who atoned for our sins through his death on the cross as the perfect Lamb of God (Isaiah 53.6; 1 John 2.2). Pray for Dudi.

For more information on the plight of persecuted Christians and how you can help, see: www.barnabasfund.org

[1] David Soakell, *Watching Over Zion*, Christian Friends of Israel, 19th October 2017.

[2] Ibid.

[3] Jerusalem News Network, 4th October 2017, quoting CBN.

[4] ASSIST News Service, 19th October 2017, quoting *The Christian Post*.

[5] JNN, 2nd October 2017, quoting Arutz-7.

CHAPTER 20 – A SOLID FOUNDATION

In searching out a memorial plaque to a Jewish relative while spending time with family in the heart of London, I marvelled at the magnificent statues paying tribute to nation builders who followed Christ. Among them were Robert Raikes, William Tyndale and General Gordon of Khartoum – men who truly denied themselves as they took up their cross to follow Jesus; and in so doing left a legacy which no amount of this world's wealth could ever match.

They had certainly taken to heart the Saviour's warning, *What shall it profit a man if he gains the whole world, but loses his soul?* along with his call to build on the rock of his words rather than on the sand without foundation (see Mark 8.36, Matthew 7.24-27).

Robert Raikes was the founder of the Sunday School movement through which generations of children were taught about the love of God through his one and only Son. Tragically, few attend these days, and fewer still have any knowledge of God's laws and commands; is it any wonder that we live in an increasingly lawless society?

William Tyndale was burnt at the stake for daring to translate the Bible into English 500 years ago – and his dying prayer was that God would open the King's eyes to its enduring truths! His prayer was answered, the Bible became the world's best-seller and Britain became a great nation built upon God's laws. Thankfully, our present Queen is already a follower of Jesus, as she makes quite clear in her annual Christmas messages. But it is the eyes of many of her subjects that need to be opened.

General Gordon won many battles for Britain before losing his life in the defence of Khartoum. He declined both a title and financial reward from the British government but, after some persuasion, accepted a gold medal inscribed with a record of his 33 military engagements. It became his most prized possession. After his death in 1885, however, it could not be found. It was only later, when his diaries were unearthed, that it was discovered how, on hearing news of a severe famine, he had sent the medal to be melted down and used to buy bread for the poor. He had written in his diary, "The last earthly thing I had in this world that I valued I have given to the Lord Jesus Christ today." [1]

Gen Gordon was a Christian who knew where his treasure lay. Are we as willing to heed Jesus' teaching not to invest in this world's treasures, but in the eternal kingdom where moths and vermin cannot destroy, nor thieves break in and steal? (See Matthew 6.19-21.)

In the shadow of his statue I found the plaque to my esteemed relative, Lt Frank de Pass, who also sacrificed his life for our freedom. A cousin of my grandmother, he was posthumously awarded the Victoria Cross – the first Jewish soldier to be so honoured – for conspicuous bravery during the early stages of World War I in November 1914. An officer with the Indian Army regiment, he led an attack on a German post under enemy fire and subsequently rescued a wounded soldier, but was killed in action not long afterwards, aged just 27.

As I turned to peer through the trees of the Thames Embankment, I was impressed by our ultra-modern skyline with its strange but interesting shapes piercing the heady atmosphere of this bustling city. The pointed, pyramid-like structure of the 98-storey Shard is uncomfortably close to what I am led to believe the Tower of Babel looked like. It certainly seems to echo the arrogant boast of the ancients about making a name for themselves with a tower that reaches the heavens. (See Genesis 11.1-9.)

But how fragile this all is, for just a few miles west stood the blackened skeleton of the 24-storey Grenfell Tower, an ugly memorial to the 72 people who perished in the 2017 inferno there – victims, it seems, of poor design and construction. When New York's 110-storey Twin Towers came crashing down at the hands of terrorists in 2001, we were understandably shocked at the depth of depravity shown by fanatical Islamists. But did we ask if God was perhaps using a ruthless people to bring us to our senses, as the prophet Habakkuk discovered to his shock in ancient times?

Of course I am in no way trying to justify the motivation of those who committed this atrocity, but the Twin Towers clearly represented the Western world's focus on material wealth, and of its greed and avarice often at the expense of the poor and needy. Having said that, the perpetrators of that terrible disaster, in which some 3,000 perished, saw it more as an attack on the West in general, and Israel in particular. After all, New York is home to more Jews than any city in the world including Tel Aviv!

Like the ruthless Babylonians of old, the terrorists hated the Jews above all. And the shocking thing was that God allowed the attack to happen, as he had done in Habakkuk's day when the Temple was destroyed and the Jews were carried off into exile.

As we have turned our backs on the God who made Britain great, the prospect of being invaded by enemies forcing us to worship foreign gods is not far-fetched. To a certain extent, it has already happened. Britain was only spared from Nazi invasion by a nationwide response to repeated calls for prayer from King George VI, the Queen's father.

Have we the spine, or the will, to resist the invading forces of evil in the gathering gloom of politically-correct immorality now threatening our land? Or have we resisted God so long that we are no longer able to distinguish good from evil?

Jesus is the cornerstone, or capstone, spoken of by Isaiah on which everything we build on depends. (See 1 Peter 2.4-12.) If we do not believe and trust in the One who is the cornerstone, the entire edifice of all that we have built our lives upon will crash to the ground, just as happened with the Jewish Temple after the people of Jerusalem rejected their Messiah. This is such an important issue that the Apostle Peter quotes Isaiah 28.16, Psalm 118.22 & Isaiah 8.14 as he urges the first century believers to focus entirely on Christ as they live out their lives. If Jesus is not our focal point, he will be our stumbling block.

But if you still have (spiritual) ears to hear, God is concerned for your soul. It is the most precious thing you own. If you store up treasure on this earth, who will have it when you are gone? I am not only addressing those on the fringe of church life, or even outside of it altogether. There are many Christians who spend far too much time concerned for the things of this world rather than pointing men and women to Christ, who alone can satisfy our souls. The cross is the way to life. Jesus said: *I am the way, and the truth, and the life; no-one comes to the Father except through me* (John 14.6). There is no other way to eternal life. Preach the cross; preach Jesus. Win souls for Him!

---

[1] *Cuckoos in the Nest* by Sam Gordon (Christian Year Publications), p123.

As Jews across Europe come under increasing fire, and the scandal of anti-Semitism continues to wreak havoc in Britain's Labour Party, there is an ever-present danger of misunderstanding as to what it is all about.

Why have Jews, and Israel in particular, become the focus of so much vilification? And what on earth is Zionism, a catch-all word generally being used in a disparaging way by opponents of the Jewish state?

Among the many unsavoury allegations of anti-Jewish sentiment surrounding Opposition Leader Jeremy Corbyn, he was recently cited as having said in a 2013 speech that Zionists in the UK had "no sense of English irony", which critics said implied they were not fully British.[1]

Quite apart from this being a nasty slur that is patently untrue – for British Jews have surely been the most loyal of minorities, contributing hugely to our success in so many fields, not least the economy – let us put that aside for a moment in a bid to unpack what is meant by Zionism.

So it is a form of insult for some – we get that – meant as a kind of synonym to describe a 'racist' people accused of stealing Palestinian land. But the reality is very different, and we need to rescue this skewed meaning from common use.

In truth, Zionism is among the most noble, holy concepts found in the English language (or any language) and those who take up its cause should be justly proud of doing so. For it is essentially a biblical concept of the place where we go up to meet with God to worship him.

Specifically, it refers to Jerusalem, God's dwelling place on earth also known as the *city of the Great King* (see Psalm 48.1f). It is a very special domain which God himself has chosen as a *resting place* (see Psalm 132.13f). So to use it as a form of insult virtually amounts to blasphemy because it involves denigration of something sacred to the Creator.

In the time of Jesus, Jews were expected to make a special pilgrimage to attend three major feasts a year – all in Jerusalem – when they would sing about going "up to Zion". The Book of Psalms is liberally strewn with joyful expressions of the holy wonder of these regular journeys. The city is built on mountains, including Mt Zion, at an elevation of nearly 3,000ft, which thus requires a stiff climb of some 4,000ft within the space of just 30 miles from the Dead Sea – which, at 1,200ft below (normal) sea level, is the lowest point on earth.

Zion describes the city of Jerusalem (Isaiah 40.9) and the nation of Israel as a whole (see Zechariah 9.13, Isaiah 60.14). And it is a place God loves (see Psalm 87.2f), having first assumed significance when King David brought the Ark of the Covenant into the stronghold of 'Zion', also named the 'City of David'.

Similarly, Zionism is a longing expressed by Jews dispersed around the world for a return to their ancient land, encapsulated in the late 19th century by Theodor Herzl and his Zionist movement that propelled the initial waves of Jewish immigration to the Holy Land. For Jews everywhere, it is like returning 'home', even if (as in most cases) their ancestors have been exiled for two thousand years. It is a divinely appointed location, and Jews have a divine right to live there.

And so Zion, as a homeland for the Jewish people, has also come to describe their right to self-determination in the re-established state of Israel. After all, Jews have prayed towards Jerusalem for thousands of years. Even the Western church, which has somewhat lost sight of its Hebraic roots, has traditionally built its altars facing east – towards Jerusalem! But there are also Christian Zionists, who support Israel's right to exist and make every effort to help them in any way they can, including sourcing the documents and finance to enable persecuted Jews to make 'aliyah' by becoming Israeli citizens.

So, more broadly speaking, Zionism is also an expression of longing by Gentiles who yearn for Emmanuel (God with us) to live among us, bringing love, joy and peace into our lives. This was clearly the sentiment behind William Blake's patriotic British anthem *Jerusalem*, expressing the desire to bring heaven[2] on earth to "England's green and pleasant land" and sung with such gusto by thousands at the Last Night of the Proms in the Royal Albert Hall every year. Though the words are a little strange, seemingly wrapped up in a belief that the British are among the lost tribes of Israel and that Jesus actually visited these hallowed shores, for which there is little evidence, it does surely echo something of a general longing for Christ to be among us.[3]

Christians United for Israel, noting the church's 'deafening' silence on the anti-Semitism scandal, points out that an attack on Zionism is also an attack on Christians.[4]

Remaining silent because of fears of engaging in what is deemed a 'political' controversy "could be one of the biggest mistakes by the church so far this century" because it is central to Christian faith and theology and "has consequences that may only be realised when the church becomes the next target of the same 'flames of hatred' that have reappeared throughout Europe".[5]

In answer to the question posed at the beginning of this section, well that is a big subject that would best be tackled in a separate book, perhaps by another author. But, in short, it is just because Jews are God's chosen people that they are so reviled. It is a fit of jealousy on the part of all who rebel against God's choice. But those who love God will love whoever he loves, especially Israel, *the apple of his eye* (see Zechariah 2.8).

[1] *Metro*, 31st August 2018.

[2] Churches have long used Jerusalem as a metaphor for heaven.

[3] Blake's poem, since put to music by Sir Hubert Parry, is apparently inspired by the apocryphal story that Jesus travelled to England in his youth, accompanied by his wealthy uncle Joseph of Arimathea. (Wikipedia)

[4] *Christians United for Israel*, 4th September 2018.

[5] Ibid.

The Second Coming

As the Western world wobbles, rumblings of earthquakes are sending out worrying signals in Israel. The two are connected, I believe. A quick succession of earthquakes have rocked parts of Galilee, significantly the region where Jesus lived and conducted much of his earth-shaking ministry which changed the world forever.

He warned that his coming again would be preceded by a number of signs including strange weather patterns – in particular an increase in earthquakes comparable to the onset of birth pains on a pregnant woman (see Matthew 24.7f). As they become more frequent and severe, we will know his coming is near.

It so happens that a very big one is due in Israel, according to geologists. When a 6.5 magnitude earthquake struck Galilee in 1837, it killed up to 7,000 people.[1]

The prophet Zechariah actually predicts that a devastating earthquake would accompany the return of the Messiah to Jerusalem. So we could be witnessing the closing stages of the present age. Are we ready to face the Judge of all mankind? Are we presiding over righteous laws?

Here in Britain, freedoms won at great cost are being jettisoned in favour of a new intolerance of those who hold the biblical views on which the country's great institutions were founded.

You could not make it up, but a man was arrested for reading the Bible outside St Paul's Cathedral (apparently at the instigation of staff there)[2] where, nearly 500 years ago, the Bishop of London burnt copies of the Bible in protest at the effrontery of William Tyndale in daring to translate God's Word into a language we could all understand (i.e. not Latin). Tyndale was later burnt at the stake, with St Paul's staff again implicated in this travesty of justice.

The man recently arrested was simply reading aloud the King James Bible, virtually the same as the one for which Tyndale was martyred – 80% of the King James New Testament is Tyndale's work.

It would seem that this incident is related to a case in Bristol concerning the arrest of a street preacher when a Crown Prosecution Service lawyer told magistrates that publicly quoting from the King James Bible "in the context of modern British society must be considered to be abusive and is a criminal matter".

It is against this background that Christian charity *Barnabas Fund* is campaigning to 'Turn the Tide' against the erosion of religious freedom and calling for a new law to protect it.

Before returning from a visit to the capital, I picked up a copy of the London *Evening Standard* and was greeted with the front page headline 'How do we turn the tide?' – referring to the latest teenage victim of the violence which has swept the city in recent years.[3]

This is another sign of the end-times. For Jesus also said: *Just as it was in the days of Noah* (which were marked by violence), *so will it be in the days of the Son of Man* (see Luke 17.26).

As the paper launched a special investigation into its causes, they are discovering – surprise, surprise – that its roots lie in what police call adverse child experiences (ACEs). In other words, in the home – which is what many of us have been saying for decades.

The home is the breeding ground either for good or evil, which is why it is so important for legislators to place the welfare of the family above all else. Instead, the family is under severe attack from all sides.

But there is hope, according to a recent survey[4] which found, among other things, that teenagers now enjoy spending more time with family. It certainly seems that they are crying out for meaning and purpose; for something bigger than themselves.

Suicide is another big killer among the young, fuelled in part by the superficial hedonism encouraged by the media which soon enough leaves its victims feeling empty and worthless. Violence is even perpetrated on a massive scale in the so-called interests of 'health' – in the UK nine million babies have been butchered before birth since the Abortion Act was passed in 1967. And we call ourselves civilised.

In addressing the protest against President Trump's visit to Britain, Opposition Leader Jeremy Corbyn said: "I wish to live in a world of peace, not of war."[5] Quite apart from the hypocrisy of such a statement from someone who referred to terror groups Hamas and Hezbollah as 'friends', and failed to effectively deal with anti-Semitism in his party, it betrays extreme naivety. After all, Mr Trump managed to get the world's most feared dictator[6] to the negotiating table. Was that not a gesture of peace?

Yes, we all want peace, and it *is* possible, but only through the Prince of Peace, Jesus Christ. Yet there is a paradox here which needs to be understood. Jesus came as the long prophesied Prince of Peace (see Isaiah 9.6) who would ultimately bring war to an end at his second appearance when people *will beat their swords into ploughshares* (Isaiah 2.4).

But he also came as one who divides. *Do not suppose that I have come to bring peace to the earth. I have not come to bring peace, but a sword* (Matthew 10.34). This was a warning that choosing him would cause division even among families because he stands as the ultimate test of whether you are for or against God. He is God come in the flesh (Colossians 2.9). Those who are for God choose him; those who are against God reject him, leaving them as enemies of both God and his disciples.

And yet he has bridged the gap between sinful man and a holy God by taking the punishment for sin we all deserve. God the Father has heaped all our sins on him so that we can enter his presence free of sin, and at peace with both God and man.

In addition, the barrier of hostility between Jew and Gentile has been broken at the cross where Jesus died; that is where you will find true peace among men. It is no fairy tale; I have seen both Jew and Arab embracing one another in reconciliation through their common love for Jesus, the Jewish Messiah, after discovering what he has done for them at the cross. (See Ephesians 2.14-18.)

Meanwhile, as Israeli residents – especially in Galilee – watch out for further ground movements with a degree of trepidation, we are reminded of what the prophet Haggai reports the Lord Almighty as saying: *In a little while I will once more shake the heavens and the earth, the sea and the dry land. I will shake all nations, and the desired of all nations* (the Messiah) *will come, and I will fill this house with glory* (Haggai 2.6f).

The New Testament Letter to the Hebrews reminds its hearers of this word, adding: *The words 'once more' indicate the removing of what can be shaken – that is, created things – so that what cannot be shaken may remain* (Heb 12.26f).

The world around us is tottering. But are *we* secure? Are *we* living in a world which cannot be shaken because of our absolute trust in the Lord?

[1] *Jerusalem News Network*, 9th June 2018, quoting the *Jerusalem Post*.

[2] *Barnabas Fund*, 10th July 2018.

[3] *Evening Standard*, 17th July 2018.

[4] Conducted by British Pregnancy Advisory Service, reported in the *Daily Mail*, 18th July 2018.

[5] *Daily Mail*, July 14th 2018.

[6] President Kim Jong-un of North Korea, in June 2018.

EPILOGUE – THE INCURABLE ROMANTIC

With traditional marriage under increasing pressure, my thoughts go back to a 'sex talk' at the 2016 Keswick Convention – a gathering of Christians in England's beautiful Lake District held every year since 1875. Professor Glynn Harrison[1] made the point that the Church's reaction to the 'sexual revolution' had been too negative and challenged his 3,000-strong audience to model the gospel through their marriages.

He is right. It is time the truths about God's perfect plan for marriage were hammered home, both practically so that people can see that it works, and theologically. The modern trend of couples 'living together' has gone unchecked partly because the alternative has not been convincing enough. Few couples seem to display sheer delight in each other.

But I truly believe that marriage is made in heaven and that there is a direct correlation between the gospel and wedded bliss. God planned the institution right at the beginning of creation, and we are told in Genesis 2.24 that a man is designed to leave his father and mother and cleave to his wife, so that the two become *one flesh* – a covenant relationship about which Jesus said … *What God has joined together, let no one separate* (Mark 10.9).

In fact, the entire Bible narrative depicts God as a loving bridegroom in pursuit of a beautiful bride. Jesus identified himself as that bridegroom (Matthew 9.15) when he was revealed to the world as the Son of God – and even now the risen, ascended and glorified Christ is waiting in heaven for his bride to make herself ready for the time of consummation when he will return to receive her in a great celebration known as the 'marriage supper of the Lamb' (see Revelation 19.9).

From Genesis to Revelation God pursues his bride, first identified as Israel, his chosen people,[2] and later expanded to include Gentiles also devoted to him. God says of Israel: *I have loved you with an everlasting love* (see Jeremiah 31.3). And even when their love for him cools, he still burns with desire for them. As we see from the Book of Hosea, God even witnesses the horror of his 'wife' prostituting herself (to other gods and idols), yet He remains faithful.

As Prof Harrison put it, the ecclesiastical phrase 'holy matrimony' is not for nothing. Marriage is "a holy way of life. We put the gospel on display to the world in our fidelity to each other. And God says, 'That's what my love is like'. You are a picture of the kind of love God has. You are saying, 'I don't do one-night stands, because God doesn't. He's always faithful'."

God does not give up on us. But he is looking for a bride who is devoted to him. When you are in love, you don't keep each other at arm's length. You draw as close as you can and gaze into each other's eyes with adoration. Indeed, this is a picture of how God appreciates worship – whether we are dancing in exuberant praise or kneeling at his feet in blissful wonder.

As lovers caress each other with groping arms and gestures, so we should be engaging with the Godhead with our entire beings. As marital consummation involves both our bodies and souls, so should our worship of Christ. Should we not love him with all our heart, soul and mind (see Deuteronomy 6.5, Matthew 22.37) and worship in spirit and in truth (see John 4.23f)? It should never be a ritual, something done at a certain place and time with the aid of a formally structured 'order of service'. We should surely surrender ourselves with abandon to his loving arms as we offer ourselves to his service and will.

But love is also practical. If we love God, we also love his law, as King David put it in Psalm 19. Carrying out God's commands – by loving him, loving our neighbour, loving justice and mercy, and living unselfishly for the benefit of others – should become part of our nature as we grow in the overflowing grace of God. A husband wishing to please his wife may need to hoover the house.

Having said that, both emotion and devotion is involved for a couple who are truly in love. And surely the Lord who created these intense feelings desires that we should also express them towards him? He is, after all, the ultimate Bridegroom, gathering together all those whose devotion is total and unwavering, unlike the foolish virgins who allowed their lamps of ardour to burn out (see Matthew 25.1-13).

Despite all today's emphasis on sex, a survey has concluded that people are actually having less of it, according to Prof Harrison. And in making the rather startling statement that "our bodies drive us to the gospel", he explained that we can never be wholly satisfied with sexual intimacy alone. We are made to desire something greater and higher, reflected by the psalmist when he writes: *As the deer pants for streams of water, so my soul pants for you, my God. My soul thirsts for God, for the living God* (Psalm 42.1f).

Yet human love is also well expressed in popular songs, the writers extolling the unbounded joy and delight of discovering, when you fall in love, that you simply cannot have enough of it. One of my favourite songs is the incredibly romantic *Some Enchanted Evening* (from the Rodgers and Hammerstein musical *South Pacific*) which tells of when, as the lyrics go, *you may see a stranger, across a crowded room, and somehow you know, you know even then, that somewhere you'll see her, again and again.*

As I mentioned earlier, my wife Linda and I met as strangers on a blind date organised by mutual friends. But God – the incurable romantic – was behind it. Six months earlier, around the time of her vision in Cana of Galilee, outlined in chapter 10, an elderly friend of mine, Denis Penhearow, rang me to apologise for not having attended the funeral of my late wife Irene as he had been ill. He was an intercessor in our church – praying on behalf of others for needs both great and small. And he told me that, as he had been praying, he had a vision of a smiling Irene reaching down from heaven with arms outstretched as if she was letting me go and urging me to marry again. Denis then added very confidently: "You will know who this (new bride) is before the end of the year (2000)."

Linda and I met on November 18th that year and were engaged before Christmas, much to the surprise of her parents. As with marriage, so with God.... If you have not yet fallen in love with Jesus, you may not have become aware that he has been consistently romancing and courting you. But he won't force himself on anyone; he wants the feeling to be mutual.

He loved you so much that he allowed wicked men to nail him to a cruel cross. But it was meant to happen because it was necessary for a perfect sacrifice to be offered for our sins. *For God so loved the world that he gave his only Son that all who believe in him should not perish but have everlasting life* (John 3.16).

As for Israel, his love for them has never waned and he longs for them to return it, as many 'Messianics' are already doing throughout the Jewish world.

When you recognise that he loves you, you surely won't be able to help responding by falling in love with Him. And when it becomes a mutual love – knowing that God loves you and you love him – it is the most amazing experience you will ever have.

He does not offer us dry and dusty formalism, or repetitive ritual, but a love that never stops flowing. And though tears may flow in this life, the future is one of unbounded joy and happiness as we bask in 'married bliss' with our Saviour and Messiah.

Meanwhile we join the rest of God's chosen people in making elaborate preparations (essentially by inviting guests – i.e. sharing the gospel) for the biggest wedding of all, when the Lion of the tribe of Judah, the Root and Offspring of David, returns for his bride (see Rev 5.5, Rev 22.16, Rev 21.2).

Come, Lord Jesus!

[1] Professor Emeritus of Psychiatry, University of Bristol, UK, who has since put his thoughts into an excellent book – *A Better Story* (IVP).
[2] See, for example, Jeremiah 2.2.

Bibliography

Boot, Joseph, *Gospel Culture*, Wilberforce Publications
Booth, Frank, *Who are the Sheep and the Goats?* Olive Press Research Paper
Drosnin, Michael, *The Bible Code*, Orion
Gordon, Sam, *Cuckoos in the Nest*, Christian Year Publications
Harrison, Prof Glynn, *A Better Story*, Inter-Varsity Press
Henderson, Geoffrey *Lewis Way – A Biography*, HTS Media
Newell, Dr Theresa, *Rev Dr Jakob Jocz*, Olive Press Research Paper
Pawson, David, *Defending Christian Zionism*, (in response to Stephen Sizer and John Stott), Anchor Recordings
Pawson, David *Unlocking the Bible*, Collins
Phillips, Melanie, *The World Turned Upside Down*, Encounter Books
Saada, Tass with Merrill, Dean, *Once an Arafat Man*, Tyndale Publishing
Sammons, Peter, *One Flesh*, Christian Publications International (what Jesus teaches about love, relationships, marriage and a lot more), available as a PDF free of charge via the Christian Publications International website.
A Celebration of God's Unfailing Love, Evangelical Sisterhood of Mary
Every Day with Jesus, CWR

By the same author

Gardner, Charles, *A Nation Reborn*, Christian Publications International
Gardner, Charles, *Israel the Chosen*
Gardner, Charles, *Peace in Jerusalem*, olivepresspublisher.com
Rochester, New York State, USA

ABOUT THE AUTHOR

Charles Gardner is a Cape Town-born journalist who began his career in Fleet Street as a London correspondent for the *South African Press Association*. He subsequently moved to Yorkshire, where he has been involved in a senior editorial capacity on a number of newspapers. He has also launched Christian publications, including the evangelistic tabloid *New Life*, and after retirement from full-time work in 2012, signed up as a volunteer with the Church's Ministry among Jewish people (CMJ). He is also author of *A Nation Reborn*, *Israel the Chosen* (Amazon) and *Peace in Jerusalem* (olivepresspublisher.com). He is married to Linda, who teaches Christianity and Judaism in Doncaster's primary schools, and has four children and nine grandchildren. He is also a regular contributor to www.prophecytoday.uk, *Heart Publications*, Jerusalem-based *Israel Today* – www. israeltoday.co.il, *Gateway News* (an online portal in South Africa) and CMJ's USA and UK websites.